Creation Is Waiting For You!

Empowering youth to be problem solvers, lights
to the world and leaders

HANNA H. ASSEFA

ISBN-10: 1519455399

ISBN-13: 978-1519455390

Cover Photo: Adobe Creative Cloud

Back page photo credit: Mihert Assefa (M-Studio)

DEDICATION

This book is dedicated to my Lord Jesus Christ and to all of those who contributed to my spiritual, mental, and physical growth. Thank you!

CREATION IS WAITING FOR YOU!

Table of Contents

CREATION IS WAITING FOR YOU!

Why I wrote this book

I have lived in both developing and developed countries. In 1996 when I was a teen, my family and I moved from Ethiopia to the United States. I have the fondest memories of growing up in Ethiopia. Though I lived a sheltered life, I was surrounded by family and friends. My middle-income earning family repeatedly drilled in my siblings and me the importance of education. As a result, we had an ongoing friendly competition with friends to get the best grades. At the same time, we had plenty of freedom to play with our friends outdoors, enjoying the tropical weather. Sadly, the gap between the poor and rich was very wide. There was extreme poverty all around. I knew a lot of bright young people who had to interrupt their education to get jobs to support their families. Some of them did not even eat three meals a day.

For the first two years of being in the United States, I not only experienced culture shock, but I also had to learn English quickly so I could communicate with Americans. Meanwhile, my parents were going through the same culture shock while working minimum-paying jobs. During this time, I had to figure out which peer group I should join, the partying group or those who were serious about their education. Fortunately the church I attended at the time helped ground me and choose the right group.

Even though I had my own struggles as a young woman, my growing wisdom in the Word helped me navigate often-confusing territory and temptation. 3 John 2 (NKJV) tells us we should prosper in all things: "Beloved, I pray that you may prosper in all things and be in health, just as your soul prospers." "All things" include spirit, soul, and body.

I do not believe, however, my peers and I were prosperous. After all, we dealt with the same problems in the church that non-Christians experience, such as teenage pregnancies, drug abuse, imprisonment, deportation, suicide, and dropping out of school. Even though I did not personally deal with these issues, I was still not living a prosperous life. I constantly worried, feared, and did not have the right image of God. I didn't believe that God was pleased with me, and that I had to serve Him to earn His love.

So while I did not leave the church, I did not live the abundant life Jesus spoke about in John 10:10 (NKJV): "The thief does not come except to steal, and to kill, and to destroy. I have come that they may have life, and that they may have it more abundantly."

Jesus came so we may all have an abundant life, where our spirits, souls and bodies are peaceful, fulfilled, and healthy, so we have everything we need to fulfill the purpose for which we are created.

Even after I finished college, however, I still did not witness this kind of life, but started teaching Sunday school nonetheless. I saw students who had so much potential fall into a downward spiral. I saw young people who had the capacity to change the world for the better, but whose lives were cut short from reaching that vision. Instead they lived like they had no hope for the future; they had no plan, no goal; they just went whichever way the wind blew; they followed the latest fashions, fads, and TV shows; they spent countless hours on social media, existing with no regard for their future. Even many who still had hope and attended the church lacked purpose, motivation, self-confidence, performed at a mediocre level at school, and struggled with their identities.

I realized our young people were in trouble and wanted to help them. So I urgently wrote this book of encourage-ment and inspiration to guide our youth to make better choices. I want them to realize they are a chosen generation that will bring solutions to the world's problems. I want to help them understand that Jesus died so they could live an extraordinary life. I want to share a message that will shatter limitations, deceptions of the enemy, low self-confidence, laziness, and distractions, a message filled with hope, purpose, and intentional living. This book is my way of bridging the gap in information by retelling familiar biblical stories in a way that young people can relate to, and providing motivation and encouragement as they struggle to find their purpose and heed their calling.

Similarly, I've observed that young people in developing countries have many issues in common with those in the United States, even though they come from different socioeconomic backgrounds. A recent BBC article titled [1]"Head-to-head: Is Africa's young population a risk or an asset?" states, "There is a strong case to be made that a young population, or a poorly managed young population, leads to instability and civil conflict." This is true in many countries because these young people have become easy targets for brainwashing with extreme ideologies, being lured into becoming child soldiers, and becoming victims of human trafficking.

To make matters worse, developing countries have an astonishing number of youth populations. [2]Sixty percent of Africa's population, for example, is under the age of 30, compared with 40 percent of the United States' population. That figure is more than 70 percent for more than half the countries in Africa, such as Uganda, Chad, Ethiopia, Nigeria, Somalia, and Kenya. These young people face the same obstacles that those in technologically advanced countries face, in addition to poverty, lack of opportunity, and evildoers who will exploit this lack. This simply compounds their problems and levels of despair.

During one of my visits to Ethiopia, I saw girls who look like they could be between ages 16 and 21 lining up by the thousands to get a Visa so they could be maids in Arab countries. These girls convert from their Christian religion to Islam just so they can earn an income to support their families. Once they get to these countries, however, they are verbally, physically, and sexually abused.

The solution to these problems is all young people becoming assets to their families, countries, and the world, regardless of where they live. This transformation starts with a proper foundation in spiritual and academic knowledge. I wrote this book to provide young people with that fundamental knowledge they need to live the abundant life Jesus promised and to give them the inspiration and desire to become a light and leaders in our world. While this book is directed at youth, anyone wishing to learn how to spiritually mentor the young people in their lives should also read this book.

Romans 8:19 (NIV) says, "For the creation waits in eager expectation for the children of God to be revealed." Creation is eagerly waiting for the children of God to manifest. It is waiting for you! Will you heed the call?

Part I

Why is Creation Waiting for you?

CREATION IS WAITING FOR YOU!

Chapter One

What is Creation?

So what is this creation that is eagerly waiting for the children of God to be revealed? Creation is everything created by God from day one to day six in the book of Genesis, and everything created by man. Genesis 1 tells us that God created the heavens and the earth; the day and the night; the sky, the land, and the seas; all the vegetation; the sun, the moon, and the stars; all the animals; and human beings. Men also created systems such as education, government, business, health, and finance.

Romans 8:19 is clear on who the creation is waiting for—the children of God. The question is, why? The answer can be easily found if you listen to the news where we hear every day about war, famine, orphans, robbery, crimes against humanity, diseases, oppression, human rights violations, human trafficking, terrorism, suicide bombers, corruption, reckless youth activities, lack of morals, drug abuse, and pollution.

While these are the world's current problems, there will be problems in the future, as well. [2]The substantial under-30 populations in African countries, for example, lack the basic resources and education needed to get jobs. As a result, unemployment is high. 52.2 percent South Africans, 42.4 percent of Tunisians, and 38.3 percent of Egyptians are unemployed youths. These are the future of Africa and whatever gets their attention gets the future of the entire continent. Because of the lack of education and employment, any bad ideology can and will engulf Africa.

The creation is eagerly waiting for the children of God to provide solutions.

CREATION IS WAITING FOR YOU!

Chapter Two

Creation is waiting for you to solve the world's problems

God created you with the potential to solve the world's problems. Will you answer the call?

When the first human, Adam, sinned against God by eating the forbidden fruit in the Garden of Eden, his spirit separated from God—this is the ultimate death of the human spirit. This affected all of Adam's offspring until Jesus came.

Romans 5:18 (NKJV) tells us, "Therefore, as through one man's offense judgment came to all men, resulting in condemnation, even so through one Man's righteous act the free gift came to all men, resulting in justification of life."

As Jesus was God's answer to Adam's fall, we are the answer to the world's problems. Our acceptance of Jesus as the savior and our belief in His death and resurrection has caused our spirits to be born again, our authority to be restored, and us to be reconciled with God.

The story of Joseph perfectly illustrates how one man can solve a problem. Joseph encountered many challenges in his life, but he manifested his problem solving skills cleverly and with faith. As the saying goes, he knew how to turn his lemons into sweet lemonade. From the sour situations he found himself in, he was able to bring forth something sweet.

Joseph had 11 brothers but he was especially loved by his father. One night, Joseph dreamed he was a leader and shared that dream with his brothers. They became so jealous of him that they threw him into a pit and later sold him as a slave to an Ishmaelite who took him to Egypt in bondage. In spite of his brothers' evil actions, which were meant to harm him, Genesis 39:2-4 (NKJV) tells us:

> "The LORD was with Joseph, and he was a successful man; and he was in the house of his master the Egyptian. And his master saw that the LORD was with him and that the LORD made all he did to prosper in his hand. So Joseph found favor in his sight, and served him. Then he made him overseer of his house, and all that he had he put under his authority."

Unfortunately, his master's wife lusted after him and nagged him to sleep with her. When Joseph refused, his master's wife wrongfully accused him and he was sent to prison. Genesis 39:21-23 (NKJV) says, however:

> "But the Lord was with Joseph and showed him mercy, and He gave him favor in the sight of the keeper of the prison. And the keeper of the prison committed to Joseph's hand all the prisoners who were in the prison; whatever they did there, it was his doing. The keeper of the prison did not look into anything that was under Joseph's authority, because the Lord was with him; and whatever he did, the Lord made it prosper."

Joseph's story takes an interesting turn, for while he was still in prison, Pharaoh, the ruler of Egypt, had a disturbing dream and could not find anyone to interpret it. He just knew the dream had great significance because of all the symbolic references it contained. *Genesis 41:1-7 says:*

> "Then it came to pass, at the end of two full years, that Pharaoh had a dream; and behold, he stood by the river. Suddenly there came up out of the river seven cows, fine looking and fat; and they fed in the meadow. Then behold, seven other cows came up after them out of the river, ugly and gaunt, and stood by the other cows on the bank of the river. And the ugly and gaunt

cows ate up the seven fine looking and fat cows. So Pharaoh awoke. He slept and dreamed a second time; and suddenly seven heads of grain came up on one stalk, plump and good. 6 Then behold, seven thin heads, blighted by the east wind, sprang up after them. And the seven thin heads devoured the seven plump and full heads. So Pharaoh awoke, and indeed, it was a dream."

The prisoners knew Joseph as a man gifted in interpreting dreams. Because one of them who was released from prison told Pharaoh about Joseph's gift, Pharaoh called upon Joseph to interpret his dream. As Joseph did so, he conveyed Egypt was going to have seven years of plenty and seven years of famine.

Joseph didn't just interpret the dream, however; he came up with a solution to the impending famine, which he described in a four-step process:

1.   Pharaoh should select a discerning and wise man to be a leader.
2.   Officers should be selected to collect one-fifth of the produce during the seven plentiful years.
3.   Grain should be stored in every city.
4.   The stored grain should be used to feed the people during the seven years of famine.

This solution pleased Pharaoh so much that he made Joseph ruler over the land of Egypt! As a result of Joseph's instruction, the Egyptians were saved from the famine. Joseph became the one man who saved many from starving to death.

But this amazing comeback story does not end there. During the crisis, Joseph was reconciled with his family and restored their prosperity. He loved his family and chose to forgive them, knowing God had preserved him for a time to use him to provide not only for his family but for all nations.

Joseph wanted his family to come and live with him and have sustainable wealth in Egypt, but he did not want them to mix with the Egyptian idol worshipers. So Joseph came up with a strategy using his God-given wisdom. In order for his family to be positioned for success, he needed to secure land, not just any land, but prime land for living and sheep grazing. He selected Goshen. To ensure his family's success in getting this prime plot of land, in Genesis 46:33-34 (NJKV), Joseph told his brothers what to say when Pharaoh summoned them:

> "So it shall be, when Pharaoh calls you and says, "What is your occupation?" that you shall say, "Your servants' occupation has been with livestock from our youth even till now, both we and also our fathers," that you may dwell in the land of Goshen; for every shepherd is an abomination to the Egyptians."

When the famine came to Egypt, Joseph started selling the grain that was purchased during the bountiful season. When the Egyptians ran out of money, Joseph started exchanging grain for their livestock. His family was to shepherd that livestock, since Egyptians despised shepherds, and his family had been given a grazing area separate from them. After the Egyptians had sold all their livestock, they returned to Joseph to sell their land and themselves in bondage to Pharaoh in exchange for food.

Toward the end of the famine, to sustain the wealth of the government, Joseph allowed the Egyptians to sow seed on land they had sold to Pharaoh, provided they give the government 20 percent of the harvest. In a masterful strategy, Joseph had successfully transferred all the wealth from the Egyptians to the government that Pharaoh had placed him in charge of, which benefitted his family as the keeper of all the livestock in the land.

Creation is waiting for people like Joseph, a man who became the catalyst for deliverance, redemption, and restoration in the lives of many, all because of his efforts and faith in the dream God placed in his heart when he was a young man. Creation is waiting for a new generation who will not only pinpoint problems, but also come up with solutions. Only then can we open greater doors and bring relief to God's creation.

You can become like Joseph; you just need the same kind of attitude he had. Problems should not cause you to give up or change direction. You can come up with creative solutions. You can train your mind not to shut down or get frustrated when you encounter obstacles. Problems are not dead ends but opportunities for growth. They will stretch your imagination and you will end up operating in potential you never knew you had.

Another important lesson we can take away from Joseph's story is that his solutions were not temporary; they had a lasting impact and affected many generations. In order to solve the fuel problems in Africa, for example, people cut down many trees. But this "solution" caused another problem, deforestation. Temporary solutions will always cause cascading issues. To avoid this trap, follow this problem-solving guide:

1. Define the problem.

    Clearly defining the problem is a critical step to solving the right problem. Ask, "What?" "Why?" "Who?" "When?" "Where?" and "How?" In the biblical example we discussed, Joseph defined the problem for Egypt as a seven-year period of prosperity followed by a seven-year period of famine.

2. Brainstorm solutions.

    It is important to be uninhibited and to come up with as many solutions to the problem as possible. Brainstorming with a group is ideal. We do not know whether Joseph brainstormed for a solution, but an ideal solution normally gets selected after contemplating many scenarios.

3. Select a Solution.

   Prayerfully select a solution that is the most likely to bring the best result. Making a list of pros and cons to any solution you come up with will help you select the best one. Joseph determined that in the years of plenty he needed to store the grain, and in the years of lack he needed to sell the grain.

4. Assign responsibilities and tasks to implement the solution.

   Define your responsibility, along with the responsibilities of others, to implement the solution. Joseph suggested that a leader, along with officers in each city, be selected to accomplish the task.

5. Continually evaluate progress and success of the solution.

   Monitor how well or how poorly the solution is working and make adjustments if needed. Also evaluate time and resources that went into implementing the solution and achieving the desired result. We know the end of Joseph's story, so we are able to evaluate his solution. It was successfully implemented on time and within budget.

The world has many problems and it is waiting eagerly with expectation for you to solve them. The steps above will guide you to come up with a solution. You cannot solve every problem but you can solve at least one problem that moves your inner being.

Questions for personal reflection:

1. What are some of the problems in creation you see around you?

2. Which of these problems are you passionate enough about to solve?

3. Use the problem-solving guide to brainstorm a solution to a current problem.

4. Which solution would you select if you had unlimited resources?

5. What can you do now to keep your passion for this issue burning?

6. What actions will you take today to develop your solution?

7. How much time do you think it will take to accomplish your vision?

CREATION IS WAITING FOR YOU!

Chapter Three

Creation is waiting for you to be the Light of the World

Matthew 5:14-16 (NKJV) clearly states, "You are the light of the world. A city that is set on a hill cannot be hidden. Nor do they light a lamp and put it under a basket, but on a lampstand, and it gives light to all who are in the house. Let your light so shine before men, that they may see your <u>good works</u> and glorify your Father in heaven."

Being the light of the world is more than an evangelical outreach term. It is more than just sharing the gospel of Jesus Christ in a dark world. We become lights to the world through "good works." When others see our good works, it will bring glory to God. Mind you, these are not just the good works we do in church. Our good works should have a far greater reach. Although religious activities are good, they may not bring glory to God if our everyday behavior is contrary to God's commands.

In Isaiah, the children of Israel thought they were doing well by participating in a day of fasting. God, however, found displeasure in their day of fasting because they were exploiting their laborers and participating in strife and wickedness. In Isaiah 58:6-7 (NKJV), God explains to them what He considers a true fast:

> "Is this not the fast that I have chosen: To loose the bonds of wickedness, To undo the heavy burdens, To let the oppressed go free, And that you break every yoke? Is it not to share your bread with the hungry, And that you bring to your house the poor who are cast

out; When you see the naked, that you cover him, And not hide yourself from your own flesh? Then your light shall break forth like the morning, Your healing shall spring forth speedily, And your righteousness shall go before you; The glory of the LORD shall be your rear guard."

God is interested in a fast that benefits others, such as loosing the bonds of wickedness, undoing heavy burdens, letting the oppressed go free, breaking yokes, offering food and shelter to the hungry and poor, and providing clothing to the naked.

We can, therefore, apply these verses through such acts as helping prostitutes get off the streets and finding them paying jobs; helping people flee from an oppressive government by assisting them with the immigration process; working to end illiteracy and lack of knowledge, and being a voice that stands up to social and economic slavery of any kind.

The good works are not limited to humanitarian efforts. Good works can be accomplished through business and policy changes as well. Inventing and selling something that will help society or discovering medicines that will cure diseases, are also good works. Some entrepreneurs give back a percentage of their profit to the community to be used for scholarship purposes or to meet other community needs. A company called TOMS is a good example of a business directly giving back to the community. TOMS gives one pair of shoes to children in developing countries when a customer buys a new pair of shoes. There are many companies that participate in this type of philanthropic model, using their business as a means.

Policies have a far reaching impact in our world. For example, 5China's one child policy prevented 400 million births since 1979. That is more than the entire population of the USA.

24

This is an example of a policy I do not personally agree with but it has had a huge impact on the footprint of the world. You can imagine then how good policies can impact the world! These are just a few examples. Whatever incites passion within you to serve others gives you the opportunity to allow God's light to shine through. This is what good works are all about and, as Isaiah 58:8-12 (NKJV) states,

"Then your light shall break forth like the morning,
Your healing shall spring forth speedily,
And your righteousness shall go before you;
The glory of the Lord shall be your rear guard.
Then you shall call, and the Lord will answer;
You shall cry, and He will say, 'Here I am.'

If you take away the yoke from your midst,
The pointing of the finger, and speaking wickedness,
If you extend your soul to the hungry
And satisfy the afflicted soul,
Then your light shall dawn in the darkness,
And your darkness shall be as the noonday.
The Lord will guide you continually,
And satisfy your soul in drought,
And strengthen your bones;
You shall be like a watered garden,
And like a spring of water, whose waters do not fail.
Those from among you
Shall build the old waste places;
You shall raise up the foundations of many
generations;
And you shall be called the Repairer of the Breach,
The Restorer of Streets to Dwell In."

In the New Testament, Jesus does not say if we do good works we will gain righteousness, healing or eternal life. Those are gifts. However, doing these activities brings great satisfaction and a legacy that impacts generation. Doing good works is as much a part of the Christian identity as being a child of God. Jesus says in Matthew 25:35-40 (NKJV):

> "...for I was hungry and you gave Me food; I was thirsty and you gave Me drink; I was a stranger and you took Me in; I was naked and you clothed Me; I was sick and you visited Me; I was in prison and you came to Me.' "Then the righteous will answer Him, saying, 'Lord, when did we see You hungry and feed You, or thirsty and give You drink? When did we see You a stranger and take You in, or naked and clothe You? Or when did we see You sick, or in prison, and come to You?' And the King will answer and say to them, 'Assuredly, I say to you, inasmuch as you did it to one of the least of these My brethren, you did it to Me.'"

As a church and as individuals we must dedicate ourselves and our resources to these types of good works. When we serve the hungry, the thirsty, the strangers, the naked, those who are sick, and the prisoners, we are serving Jesus.

The good works we do give light. What are some of the attributes of these good works?

1. They give light in the darkness.
   Light is meant to illuminate the darkness. We need to take our light from the church and go out into the darkness to give our light. I am not saying we need to abandon the church, but we should be using it to refuel and receive training to go back out into the world of darkness in order to bring light.

2. They cannot be hidden.
   Luke 8:18 (NKJV) says, "No one, when he has lit a lamp, covers it with a vessel or puts it under a bed, but sets it on a lampstand, that those who enter may see the light. For

nothing is secret that will not be revealed, nor anything hidden that will not be known and come to light...."

If you are in a big, dark auditorium and someone turns on a flashlight, you will see it. Light cannot be hidden. Unfortunately, most people are hiding their light so the world cannot see it. Remaining hidden, however, is counterintuitive to being a Christian. God wants us to show His light to the world so we can reveal His goodness to others.

Why do we hide our light? It is because we fear people and rejection, or because we're insecure? Those could be part of the reason but we also hide our light because we do not know our own value or the power we have inside us. If we genuinely believe we have something important to share, if we believe we have the light of the world Himself living inside us, then why are we hiding? Why are we limiting ourselves to the four corners of the church when the world is our domain? We must seek every opportunity to be a light to the world.

3. They make everything known around them.
   Nothing will be hidden next to a light. It will be known and revealed. When we turn our light on, we will see a path and be able to navigate through the darkness to our intended destiny. When we take one step in faith, God will reveal the next step.

4. They must be displayed for maximum effect.
   If the source of light in a house is a lamp, it needs be displayed in the center of the room where it has the greatest potential to push out the darkness. God's children need to be a light everywhere: in the world, in the city, in the house, and before men. As lights to the world, we

should be at the forefront (or the center), so others will see our good works and praise our Father in heaven.

We need to be in an environment where our light will have the greatest impact. If we are inhibited or limited, it is time to find another environment where we can be effective.

Questions for personal reflection:

1. What are some examples of the darkness you see around you?

2. What types of good works will be able to provide a light into that darkness?

3. What are some of the things that are making you hide instead of shine?

4. What does scripture say about those limitations?

5. How can you be a light where you are today?

6. How can you be a light globally?

CREATION IS WAITING FOR YOU!

Chapter Four

Creation is waiting for you to be a leader

Leadership expert John C. Maxwell popularized the statement, "Leadership is an influence." Most Christians, however, have a very limited view of leadership. They think leaders are only those who preach, who are articulate speakers, or who are CEOs or managers. If a person doesn't naturally have these or other obvious leadership traits, Christians often automatically exclude themselves from leadership consideration, and by extension, exclude ourselves from influencing our community, country, and generation. How then can we complain about our degenerated culture and politics?

As Christians we are all called to lead in some areas and follow in others, depending on our passion and gifts. Creation is desperately waiting for people who will bring a positive influence to the world. But it starts with knowing you have the capability to lead. Being a leader is not limited to a few chosen people. You can be a change maker. Leadership was God's intention when he created you. Genesis 1:27-28 (NKJV) says:

> "So God created man in His own image; in the image of God He created him; male and female He created them. Then God blessed them, and God said to them, "Be fruitful and multiply; fill the earth and subdue it; have dominion over the fish of the sea, over the birds of the air, and over every living thing that moves on the earth.""

God created us in His likeness, which means we have inherited His character, and one of His character traits is lead According to the scripture above, God has also blessed fruitful, multiply, subdue, and have dominion over th

You can see in our world today how humans dominate nature by building massive bridges, dams, and buildings and finding ways to live in harsh weather conditions. Mankind accomplished these things when they tapped into their God-given leadership and creative skills.

God also created us to be fruitful and multiply, not only by having children, but by having ideas, as well. Our ideas can also multiply and influence many people. Martin Luther King Jr's "I have a dream" speech, for example, and his then-revolutionary ideas for freedom, developed new laws and policies that helped bring an end to segregation. His fundamental beliefs, his hope, and his vision for change are echoed in his words:

> "Now, I say to you today my friends, even though we face the difficulties of today and tomorrow, I still have a dream. It is a dream deeply rooted in the American dream. I have a dream that one day this nation will rise up and live out the true meaning of its creed: "We hold these truths to be self-evident, that all men are created equal.""

Dr. King's leadership influence rippled through society and brought the freedom that we enjoy today after many decades.

Let us look at Esther and Nehemiah as biblical examples of leadership.

Esther

God gave Esther favor and grace. Her parents died and she was raised by her cousin, Mordecai. She came from a humble background, yet she was selected to be the wife of King Ahasuerus, over all the other young ladies in the country. Because of her marriage, she was lifted up to a much greater position and influence. After some time, Mordecai informed

Esther of an evil plot by a man called Haman, (who was above all princes of the land) to kill the entire Jewish population. Esther knew she had to use her influence to stop Haman's scheme. Mordecai, in his wisdom, advised Esther that perhaps she was given favor with the King and a top position in the country for "such a time as this" (Esther 4:13, NKJV). Mordecai went on to tell Esther that if she did not take action, God would raise up someone else to bring salvation to the Jewish people.

In those days, the policy of the kingdom was that a woman could not enter the court of the king unless she was summoned. The punishment for disobeying this command was death. To deal with her dilemma, Esther waited for God to guide her by fasting and praying for three days. After three days, she courageously went into the king's presence, and by God's grace she was welcomed. She twice invited the king and the evil man, Haman, to a banquet and used diplomacy to soften the king's heart. In both instances, the king was pleased and repeatedly asked her to name her petition. He felt so favorably toward her that he promised to give her half his kingdom. During the second banquet, she presented her petition to save her people from genocide, and Haman's evil plot to kill her people was reversed.

Esther had to face her fears and fulfill her destiny or risk turning her back on God. She chose the former. What made Esther a leader was that she did not forget her beginnings –she was very connected to her community. She also knew the policy of the kingdom and she knew how to approach the king to reverse the entire plot.

What we learn from Esther is that influential leaders are not passive. If she had been passive, her people would have been killed or God would have used someone else to save them. Either way, she would have missed the opportunity to be a solution. Martin Luther King, Jr., asks us to consider that "He who passively accepts evil is as much involved in it as he who helps to perpetrate it. He who accepts evil without protesting against it is really cooperating with it." This statement is hard to swallow but it is true. Being silent or ignoring issues as if they do not exist is not a characteristic of a true leader. Issues must be faced head on and solved.

The story of Esther also teaches us that leaders are connected to their communities. They know the issues at hand and they try to be a solution to their communities. Who better understands a community than the people who belong to it? When Esther's class, income, and fame changed, she did not forget her people. It is important for us to realize that perhaps we are in a better position than our community members, peers, family, or countrymen is to be a solution in their time of need.

Moreover, leaders may face risks similar to those Esther encountered. Dealing with risk is unavoidable, but not taking action because of the fear of risk will inhibit our impact in the world. We should take calculated risks, and "not put all our eggs in one basket." This is where prayer and fasting come into play because they will transform risks into opportunities. Prayer will change failure into victory. Leaders, therefore, will need to pray and depend on God for guidance and favor. When God's favor floods us, we need to remember where it came from. God doesn't give us favor with people or special talents just for ourselves. He wants us to use them to serve others and positively influence our world.

Nehemiah

Nehemiah is one of the greatest project managers and nation builders in the Bible. One of the most commonly known scriptures is Nehemiah 2:20 (NKJV): "...The God of heaven Himself will prosper us; therefore we His servant will arise and build...." It all started when Nehemiah heard about the distress and reproach of God's creation when he was King Artaxerxes' cupbearer. He heard, "...The survivors who are left from the captivity in province are there in great distress and reproach. The wall of Jerusalem is also broken down, and its gates are burned with fire" (Nehemiah 1:3, NKJV).

When
~~What~~ he heard that Jerusalem was falling apart, he mourned, fasted, and prayed for many days. We hear a lot of distressful news every day. Unfortunately we have become so desensitized that it does not even bother us. Or even if it does, we feel powerless to change it and resign ourselves from doing anything about it. Nehemiah, however, was burdened by the news and he fasted and prayed to figure out what he needed to do.

We cannot solve every problem we see in the news, but some news really tugs at our hearts. Some issues may bother us more than others. There are people who cry every time they hear about human trafficking news; others are sleepless when they see orphaned kids; and there are those who consistently think about proper policies and government systems. If you are passionate about an issue, then it is you who will need to do something about it. It is not complicated. An angel does not need to come down from heaven to summon you, nor do you need a prophecy about it.

It is important to pray, however, to get guidance and favor in solving the problem you are passionate about. Prayer becomes easy once you decide on the issue you want to solve. Like your work, if someone assigns you an issue to solve, then you will dig deeper to uncover more about it and come up with a solution. But if solving a particular issue is not your divinely assigned task, or you did not take ownership of it, then you have no attachment to it and will not invest the time to come up with creative solutions.

Taking ownership to solve a particular problem is an essential next step after being inspired to address the issue. We be careful not to wait for somebody else to solve the problems we are passionate about. Imagine if Nehemiah decided the problem he was burdened with was too big for him to solve and wanted another prominent Jewish leader to step up. We would have never heard this incredibly triumphant story because it would not have occurred. Solving creation's problems will make you a history maker, allow you to leave a legacy in society, and carve the way for you to reveal your God-given greatest potential.

Once this mental burden and passion to restore Jerusalem was in Nehemiah's heart, he prayed for the forgiveness of his people, who were scatted all over the world because of their disobedience. He also prayed for success in what he planned to do, as well as favor before the king: "...let your servant prosper this day, I pray, and grant him mercy in the sight of this man" (Nehemiah 1:11, NKJV). Prayer opens doors. It causes favor, opportunity, and provision to meet. Nehemiah found favor before the king and the opportunity was created for him to ask for permission to go to Jerusalem with the necessary provision.

In school we are taught that every goal should be SMART: S-simple, M-Measurable, A-attainable, R-Relevant, and T-Time bound. Nehemiah's goal was simple; to rebuild the walls of Jerusalem. The results were visually measurable. His goal was attainable and relevant. Importantly, his goal had time sensitivity. Nehemiah 2:6 (NKJV) says, "...so it pleased the king to send me; and I set him a time."

Setting a deadline to finish a task is important. Many people say, "Someday I will do this!" but they never get around to it because they have no timeframe to complete it and something else always becomes a priority. Nehemiah finished the walls of Jerusalem within 52 days. He did not do it by himself. If you read the book of Nehemiah, you can see his amazing project-management skills. He had several teams that built different gates: One team built the Sheep Gate, another built the Fish

Gate, another built Old Gate, another repaired the walls, and so on.

Getting people to support your vision is one of the skills needed for success. Nehemiah clearly outlined his vision by proclaiming in Nehemiah 2:17 (NKJV) "...Then I said to them, 'You see the distress that we are in, how Jerusalem lies waste, and its gates are burned with fire. Come and let us build the wall of Jerusalem, that we may no longer be a reproach.'" The people supported his vision by saying in Nehemiah 2:18 (NKJV) "... 'Let us rise up and build.' Then they set their hands to this good work."

You must not forget that a God-given vision or goal also has its challenges. Nehemiah was challenged before he started his project, during his project ,and after his project. How he handled these challenges made him the successful leader he is to us today. When you share your ideas with others, they may laugh at you or look down at you because they think you do not have the capacity to accomplish a particular task. They may even become jealous of you because they are competing with you. Nehemiah had naysayers named Sanballat and Tobiah who laughed at and despised him: "But when Sanballat the Horonite, Tobiah the Ammonite official and Geshem the Arab heard of it they laughed at us and despised us..." (Nehemiah 2:19, NKJV).

When I chose to major in Computer Science, quite a few people told me it was not something they thought I could do, so they advised me to change my major. Because of their prejudices, they did not think a woman, let alone a black woman, had the capacity to succeed in the technical field. Science and Engineering are still male-dominated fields—I know many capable young women who changed their majors due to the discouragement of others and a lack of role models. By God's grace, I successfully completed my major despite these obstacles.

We all have a Sanballat and Tobiah in our lives who continually try to discourage us and make us question our ability. When that happens, we must respond like Nehemiah by pointing out that it is not only our skills, but by God's grace that we will accomplish our goals. This is why Nehemiah 2:20 (NKJV) says: " ...The God of heaven Himself will prosper us; therefore we His servant will arise and build...." Nehemiah declared he would work and that God would prosper his work. He relied on God's grace to help him accomplish what he started.

When his enemies saw the wall was halfway completed, they kicked in their strategy to stop Nehemiah by conspiring to attack him. Nehemiah 4:7 (NKJV) says, "[When they] heard the walls of Jerusalem were being restored and the gaps were beginning to be closed, that they became angry, and all of them conspired together to come and attack Jerusalem and create confusion."

Nehemiah however, got creative with his solution. He encouraged his team by saying in Nehemiah 4:14 (NKJV), "...Do not be afraid of them. Remember the Lord, great and awesome, and fight for your brethren, your sons, your daughters, your wives, and you houses." It was a great motivational speech to show the people to fight for something greater than themselves.

Moreover, Nehemiah adjusted his plan based on the new challenge: "so it was from that time on that half of my servants worked at construction, while the other half held the spears, the shields, the bows, and wore armor and the leaders were behind all the house of Judah. Those who built on the wall, and those who carried burdens, loaded themselves so that with one hand they worked at construction, and with the other held a weapon" (Nehemiah 4:16-17, NKJV). The workers were so determined they did not even take off their clothes except to wash them during the project.

Tobiah and Sanballat did not give up trying to stop Nehemiah's efforts, however. In fact, they sent him a letter four times to try to lure him and kill him and sent a false prophet to him. All of his enemy's strategies, however, did not work and Nehemiah's workers were able to complete the project successfully.

We can learn so much about leadership from Nehemiah. Here are seven leadership principles we can take away from his story:

1. Figure out what you are passionate about. What issue do you want to solve?
2. Own it and be the point person.
3. Pray for guidance, success, favor, and provision.
4. Use S.M.A.R.T goals.
5. Recruit people who agree with your vision and continually champion the cause.
6. Organize and delegate.
7. Know it is not going to be easy.
   a. Rely on God's grace to help you accomplish your vision.
   b. Motivate your team.
   c. Come up with new strategies when problems arise.

Esther and Nehemiah are just two examples of many leaders in the Bible who influenced their generation. They made a significant positive impact for their people and country. You, too, can be a positive influence. Don't hesitate when the opportunity arises and continually develop your skills. Once a person knows he or she is created to be a leader, then the next step is for that person to understand which sphere he or she is to influence.

There are seven spheres of cultural influence according to Bill Bright, founder of Campus Crusade: religion, family, education, government, business, media and art, and entertainment. Most Christians' influence is only in the church; however, each area will need leaders who will be able to positively influence their generation. Imagine a government that is just, media that is uplifting and positive, and a business that is profitable in a fair way. This will not happen if Christians fold their hands and let others impose their agendas upon the world. This is why creation is waiting for you so you can be influential in the domain where you are gifted. Are you ready?

Questions for personal reflection:

1. Before reading this chapter, did you consider yourself as a leader?

2. What idea do you have that can influence generations, governments, businesses, or churches?

3. Are there any areas you are passive about instead of actively participating in?

4. What are the needs of your community?

5. Using the seven leadership principles from the story of Nehemiah, write down what you can do to solve your community problem or other problems you are passionate about.

CREATION IS WAITING FOR YOU!

Part II

What is preventing you from being revealed?

CREATION IS WAITING FOR YOU!

What is preventing you from being revealed?

The major obstacle holding back the youth from being revealed so they can be a solution to a problem, a light, and a leader, is a lack of knowledge. Hosea 4:6 (NKJV) says, "My people are destroyed for lack of knowledge." This lack of knowledge is both academic and spiritual.

There is a tendency to separate academic education and spiritual education. Formal education is considered secular and biblical teaching to be spiritual. Both are important. It does not bring glory to God to be very spiritual while academically being very poor. Jesus came so we would prosper in all aspects of our lives. 3 John 1:2 (NKJV) says, "Beloved, I pray that you may prosper in all things and be in health, just as your soul prospers." True success is when your soul, spirt, mind and body prosper.

Academic knowledge

Academic knowledge is important in order for the youth to be a solution to the world's problems. Unfortunately, many young people drop out of high school or decide not to pursue higher education. There are many reasons for this, but one primary reason is their lack of knowledge regarding the importance of pursuing higher education. Educated youth will be a blessing to their families, churches, communities, countries, and future generations. Education is one of the keys for successful living.

Nelson Mandela said, "Education is the most powerful weapon which you can use to change the world." Changing the world starts with your education. Taking your education seriously and using every opportunity you receive in school to continue learning is an investment that will keep paying off for a long time. The more you invest in educating yourself, the more valuable your skills will be and the greater your power to generate income and influence.

The book of Daniel shows us the qualities a ruling king desires in a younger generation. In Daniel's time, the king had very specific requirements for young men who wanted to serve in his court. He wanted men who had an aptitude for learning, and who were well-informed and quick to understand. Daniel, Hananiah, Mishael and Azariah had such characteristics, and, as a result, many opportunities were opened to them. Daniel 1:3-4 (NIV) says:

> "Then the king ordered Ashpenaz, chief of his court officials, to bring into the king's service some of the Israelites from the royal family and the nobility— young men without any physical defect, handsome, showing aptitude for every kind of learning, well informed, quick to understand, and qualified to serve in the king's palace. He was to teach them the language and literature of the Babylonians."

Having an aptitude for every kind of learning includes both formal education and informal learning. You can be a well-rounded, well-read, and well-educated person if you supplement your education in school with reading a variety of books. Being well-informed requires you to be intentional in your personal development, constantly seeking opportunities to learn and grow. Creation needs people like that, not just on a local level but on the global level, as well.

The source of Daniel's and his friends' knowledge and understanding was God, as confirmed in Daniel 1:7 (NKJV): "To these four young men God gave knowledge and understanding of all kinds of literature and learning. And Daniel could understand visions and dreams of all kinds."

Even when they were tested, they were found to be ten times better than the wise men from the entire kingdom (v.20). God cares about your education. You can ask God in prayer for the same greater knowledge and understanding He gave Daniel and his friends.

Daniel not only had favor with God but he also distinguished himself from others. Due to his pursuit of excellence in everything he did, great opportunities opened up for him. Daniel 6:3 (NKJV) says, "Now Daniel so distinguished himself among the administrators and the satraps by his exceptional qualities that the king planned to set him over the whole kingdom." If you excel in your education, great opportunities will open up for you. Continue to distinguish yourself, work hard, and you will see the results. Education will not only change your life but equip you to help change others, as well.

Questions for personal reflection:

1. What is your current educational level?

2. What can you do now to add to your current educational level?

3. What is your long-term educational goal?

4. How can you groom your aptitude for learning?

5. What action can you take every day to be a well-informed citizen?

Spiritual knowledge

Spiritual knowledge is just as important as academic knowledge in order for you to manifest as a solution to the world. Many young people lack the knowledge that they are created for a greater purpose. They do not know who they are or their value to God. They are not able to envision the big picture of their existence. When you understand the fundamental truth—that God created you uniquely with a divine design for your life in mind—you will live a life that is intentional, purpose driven, and focused. This knowledge will empower you to say "No" to peer pressure, to destructive behaviors, and to addictive substances. Temporary acceptance and fleeting happiness will become mediocre compared with the prize waiting for you at the end of the race.

The following chapters describe important spiritual understandings that will help you release your potential so creation can benefit from your manifestation.

CREATION IS WAITING FOR YOU!

Chapter Five

God is not angry with you

Did you know this? I used to think He was angry with me.

Growing up, I had a distorted view of God. I pictured a God who was pleased with me on the days I read the Bible, prayed, and behaved myself, and was angry with me on the days I failed to do these things or keep all the dos and don'ts of the commandments. For me, church was not a place of joy and peace—quite the opposite. I remember every Sunday before going to church, I felt choked by condemnation. I thought I had to be perfect and holy before I went to church, but I just couldn't be that good. Compared with a perfect God, I was always full of flaws and coming up short.

I don't know how I got this impression. However it happened, it filled me with guilt. But when I saw a true picture of God, I was healed.

This true picture of God came when I better understood Jesus. Through Scripture, I learned the reason Jesus came was *not* because God was angry with humanity and wanted to judge us. Jesus came because He loves us and wants us *not* to perish but to have everlasting life with Him. An often-quoted Scripture, John 3:16–17 (NKJV) says:

> "For God so loved the world that He gave His only begotten Son, that whoever believes in Him should not perish but have everlasting life. For God did not send His Son into the world to condemn the world, but that the world through Him might be saved."

If you trust in Jesus Christ as your Savior, you are free from condemnation for sins, mistakes, and regrets.

Romans 8:1 (NKJV) states it another way, "There is therefore now no condemnation to those who are in Christ Jesus, who do not walk according to the flesh, but according to the Spirit."

When God sees us, He sees His perfect Son, Jesus Christ, who made us acceptable by taking all our sins upon Himself on the cross. Through Jesus, we are reconciled to God. His love does not change based on our performance. It is unconditional. Nothing can separate us from the love of God. Nothing.

God is not angry with you. He loves you. You may say to yourself, "I have made the same mistake several times. How can God *not* be angry with me?" It is because the blood of Jesus Christ is mightier than your mistakes and can blot out all your sins. Ask for forgiveness and He will forgive you. Not only that, but He has given you His grace and the Holy Spirit to help you overcome all your weaknesses. The more you concentrate on the love of God, the less attractive the desires of the world become. Remember, God is with you for the long haul of your transformation. His vision for you is as big as eternity, and He will help you. Please don't run away from His love because you feel you are not perfect. When you fall, run *to* Him!

Knowing you can—and should—run to Him when you fall is key. This knowledge is important for you to become all God created you to be because then, whenever you mess up, you will not abandon Christ. If you wallow in feeling unworthy, bad, fearful, and undeserving of God's love, your spiritual growth will stop and it will damage your relationship with your Father. The worse you feel inside, the more you will pull away from God. You may *feel* as if you should run from Him, but that is a *lie* the enemy designed to eat up your potential, your time, and your youth and to put you in bondage.

You were not created for bondage—you were created to live in freedom! The secret to living free from sinful behavior is to understand the love of God, to know who you are in Christ, and to rely on the grace of God to live a Christ-like life. Beloved, God is not angry with you, and He will never leave you for any reason. Hebrews 13:5 (NKJV) says, "For He Himself has said, 'I will never leave you nor forsake you.'"

Questions for personal reflection:

1. When do you feel condemnation? What is the solution?

2. How do you see God?

3. If you view God as angry, hard to please, distant, harsh...etc., replace each negative view with a positive view based on scripture.

4. What do you need to do if you fail? What knowledge are you missing that is causing you to fail?

5. What steps do you need to take to live free from sinful behaviors?

Chapter Six

Depend on God's grace

The grace of God is a topic that is easily misunderstood. Some do not teach it since they think it gives people a license to sin. Some teach it without fully understanding what it means and people become misguided as a result. But when you correctly understand God's grace, you will feel greatly liberated.

Put simply, grace means unmerited favor, a favor that does not come with performance. Ephesians 2:8-9 (NKJV) tells us, "For by grace you have been saved through faith, and that not of yourselves; it is the gift of God, not of works, lest anyone should boast."

The grace of God reminds us that we are righteous because of Jesus, which means we have a right standing with God. It is hard for us to say "I am righteous" because we look at ourselves and see all our weaknesses. It is Jesus who makes us righteous in spite of our shortcomings. The grace of God also helps us if we fall. When we return to God with true repentance, it is His grace that accepts us and helps us not be tortured by past mistakes. He is the one who gives us the confidence we have to stand before Him as his children instead of feeling unworthy.

We can apply grace in every part of our lives. In fact, Paul tells us it was because of God's grace that he was able to write two-thirds of the New Testament and to preach the Good News to more people than the other disciples. 1 Corinthians 15:10 (NKJV) says, "But by the grace of God I am what I am, and His grace toward me was not in vain; but I labored more abundantly than they all, yet not I, but the grace of God which was with me. "

The grace of God helps us be better people, students, spouses, moms, dads, teachers, etc. When we understand the grace we have received, we in turn become gracious to others. Grace is the power source we plug into to be a better "us."

The intention of this chapter was not to provide loopholes for people to live sinful lives but rather to discuss what grace truly means for those who genuinely want to live the Christian life. It is for those who love the Lord and want to live lives that please God. Romans 6:11-15 (NKJV) says:

> "Likewise you also, reckon yourselves to be dead indeed to sin, but alive to God in Christ Jesus our Lord. Therefore do not let sin reign in your mortal body, that you should obey it in its lusts. And do not present your members as instruments of unrighteousness to sin, but present yourselves to God as being alive from the dead, and your members as instruments of righteousness to God. For sin shall not have dominion over you, for you are not under law but under grace. What then? Shall we sin because we are not under law but under grace? Certainly not!"

As the scripture shows, sin will not have dominion over us if we understand grace. We are dead to sin but alive to God in Christ. It means the person that used to sin has died with Christ and the person we are now is a new creation that walks in righteousness. It is not our nature sin anymore.

On the other hand those who want to live a pleasing life to God go to the other extreme by attempting to please God with their own will power. They say things like, "I am going to pray for one hour every day"; "I am going to finish reading the Bible in one year"; "I am not going to be angry anymore"; or "I am only going to confess positive words." The problem is their will power lets them down. They might be motivated for a week ily to find their motivation gone the second week. In fact, the bible defines this flesh performance to please God as falling from grace. (Galatians 5:4)

Philippians 3:3 (NKJV), tells us not to have confidence in the flesh. If we are able to pray, read the word, be patient, and confess faith-filled words, it is all by the grace of God. The moment we put confidence in the flesh, it will let us down. That fact is unchangeable. But those who tap into the power of grace will subdue the flesh and live lives pleasing to God. When we understand grace, we will live victorious and consistent lives that align with the word of God.

Christianity does not end after we accepted Christ as our savior. The Christian life requires we work out our salvation; be imitators of God; love our neighbors as ourselves; love God with all our being; love our wives as Christ loved the church; and develop the fruits of the Spirit such as love, joy, peace, longsuffering, kindness, goodness, faithfulness, gentleness, self-control, etc. All of these things can only be accomplished by the grace of God.

So in order to be a solution to a problem, a light to the world, and a leader, you must consistently be conscious of the grace of God. By the grace of God, you can do it.

Questions for personal reflection:

1. What is Grace of God?

2. Do you believe you are righteous or do you have a problem confessing it? Why?

3. How will the grace of God empower you to be a solution to the world?

4. What can you accomplish with the grace of God?

Chapter Seven

Be a doer

One of the main reasons the children of God are not revealed is inaction: they're talkers, hearers, or observers instead of doers. Our society recognizes the doers, not to the dreamers. The world makes room for the doers, not the hearers. It admires the doers instead of the talkers. The talkers impress people, but they don't influence them unless they show their dreams through action. Acting upon your vison will demand respect. James 1:22 (NKJV) commands, "But be doers of the word, and not hearers only, deceiving yourselves."

This scripture may make you question whether you are a hearer or a doer. It encourages us to be "doers of the word," but that is difficult for us if we procrastinate. Our spiritual understanding must improve, benefit, and excel in our daily lives.

Unfortunately, the Facebook and Instagram generation promotes observers instead of doers. Those who watch other people while they live, eat, or vacation are only hearers who deceive themselves. I am not against the social media culture because it has brought a lot of great benefits. In fact, the gospel of Jesus Christ will need to be presented using all the technology we have! But spending a significant amount of time on social media with no purpose is just as bad as watching too much TV. This "bad habit" can stop young generations from doing a lot of creative things.

American business woman Mary Kay Ash said, "There are three types of people in this world: those who make things happen, those who watch things happen, and those who wonder what happened." Let us be children of God who make things happen; let us be action-oriented people who do not procrastinate.

Proverbs 18:16 (NKJV) says: "A man's gift makes room for him, And brings him before great men." Your gift will make room for you and will bring you before great men. Simply talking about your gift or dreaming about what you will do with your gift will not make room for you. But producing something using your gift will make room for you and will bring you before great men.

Unfortunately, some people with great potential say things like, "One day I will write a book"; "One day I will record my music"; or "One day I will start my own business"; but their potential will not actualize unless they do something about it. Be a doer of your dream, not just a talker, hearer, or watcher. If you have a dream, then like the Nike's shoe slogan says, "Just do it."

Questions for personal reflection:

1. List all the goals you have that you want to accomplish someday.

2. List some things you do that do not contribute to achieving your dreams and that you can reduce or eliminate completely. Example: You can reduce two hours of TV or social media to 30 minutes.

3. List the tasks that need to be completed for each goal and start doing them daily or weekly.

4. Ask a family member or friends to keep you accountable for your progress.

5. Plan how you will celebrate when you accomplish your goals. This is a great motivator.

CREATION IS WAITING FOR YOU!

Chapter Eight

Overcome fear, inferiority and insecurity

Feelings of fear, inferiority or insecurity prevent the children of God from being revealed. It makes them live below their potential and settle for less than God's best. How can we overcome this mortal enemy that is holding us back every time we are inspired to do something great? Let us learn from Gideon's life in Judges Chapter 6, which tells us the people of Israel were oppressed by their enemy for seven years. It explains their oppression as follows:

> "So it was, whenever Israel had sown, Midianites would come up; also Amalekites and the people of the East would come up against them. Then they would encamp against them and destroy the produce of the earth as far as Gaza, and leave no sustenance for Israel, neither sheep nor ox nor donkey." (Judges 6:3-4, NKJV)

In the midst of this oppression, Gideon was hiding, threshing wheat in the wine press because he was too insecure to do it in the open. His feelings of fear, inferiority and insecurity were caused by the oppression of the enemy. When people are repeatedly attacked in the same areas of weakness, it debilitates their morale and sends them into hiding. As you can see from the scripture, Israel was attacked in the same way for seven years. When the harvest time arrived, the Midianites came and devoured everything. So Gideon not only chose to hide, but he also settled for less. He was threshing wheat in a wine press, which is a smaller area than a wine threshing floor. He only lived to survive.

In his state of vulnerability, the angel of the Lord came and addressed him as a courageous man in Judges 6:12 (NKJV):

"The Lord is with you, you mighty man of valor!" Imagine Gideon's confusion! The way God addressed him did not resonate with him at all, for his response in Judges 6:13 (NKJV) indicates he felt abandoned by God:

> "O my lord, if the Lord is with us, why then has all this happened to us? And where are all His miracles which our fathers told us about, saying, 'Did not the Lord bring us up from Egypt?' But now the Lord has forsaken us and delivered us into the hands of the Midianites."

Even after God assured him that He would be with him, Gideon was still not convinced. Further along in the scripture, Gideon reminds God that his clan is the least and he is the most insignificant person in his family. He was so insecure, that even after he decided to heed God's will for him, he repeatedly asked for proof that God really meant to use him to deliver the Israelites from their enemy. But God was patient with Gideon, and after a while Gideon put his confidence in the Lord and defeated his country's mighty enemy with just three hundred soldiers.

Gideon's story is not unusual. We have all been guilty of doubting God—of being insecure about His love and care for us. When we are oppressed, we feel fearful, inferior and insecure. We avoid fellowship with others. We work for mere survival, not for an abundant life. We feel helpless and abandoned by God. Even if we hear a comforting word, we come up with millions of ways why it will not solve *our* problem. We get plagued by doubt. What is the solution?

Here are a few guidelines for resolving this type of inner conflict:

1. Realize the oppression is from the enemy.

Recognizing the source of the issue is the number one step to the solution. Whether our feelings of inferiority and insecurity grew up with us or just suddenly attacked us, their root cause is the enemy of our soul. The devil does not want us to realize our God-given potential, because he knows we are created in God's image and character. The devil is the only one who does not want us to accomplish something great.

We are children of God, and oppression has no authority in our lives. We need to command it to leave us in the name of Jesus. We also need to remind ourselves how God sees us—as mighty men or women of valor and courage.

2. Realize your competence does not come from your own strength.

2 Corinthians 3:4-6 (NKJV) says, "And we have such trust through Christ toward God. Not that we are sufficient of ourselves to think of anything as being from ourselves, but our sufficiency is from God, who also made us sufficient as ministers of the new covenant, not of the letter but of the Spirit; for the letter kills, but the Spirit gives life."

God is our sufficiency. Our competence comes from Him. Whatever we accomplish in life, we do so by the grace of God. We need to look to God, therefore, to help us achieve our goals. If we look to ourselves, we will only see our shortcomings and give up.

As I said earlier, even Paul, who wrote two-thirds of the New Testament and traveled to many places to preach the gospel, credited his accomplishment to the grace of God in 1 Corinthians 15:10 (NKJV): "But by the grace of God I am what I am, and His grace toward me was not in vain; but I labored more abundantly than they all, yet not I, but the grace of God which was with me." Paul accomplished more than the other disciples because he relied on the grace of God rather than his own ability. Fear, inferiority and insecurity emotions make us look at ourselves, but when we look at God we accomplish so much more.

3. Remember that you are valuable to God.

I have met many people who have low self-confidence because they think their value comes from their educational level, their job, their bank account or the number of friends they have. When these things are not present they feel extreme insecurity. The world values you based on the things you have and what you have achieved but your true value is based on the One who reconciled you with God. His name is Jesus. Therefore, you are valuable and you have great honor before God's sight. There is nothing too impossible for you to get or to achieve. Do not give up or lower your standards in life.

4. Know that you are unlimited because there is a limitless power within you.

Gideon started with a thirty-two thousand person army to fight the enemy that came like "swarm of locusts". But God told him to reduce the army to just three hundred. God did not want the people of Israel to boast on the strength of their numbers. He also wanted them to realize greater is He who is with them than a multitude of enemies. The bible tells us in 1 John 4:4 (NKJV) "You are of God, little children, and have overcome them, because He who is in you is greater than he who is in the world." There is a greater power within us than the opposition in the world. The Word also tells us we have overcome the world. It means our victory is a done deal. The end of our book has been written and it says we will finish in victory. Amen!

It is with this attitude of victory that you can also overcome fear. Fear has a tendency to multiply everything by zero. When a number is multiplied by zero, its result is zero. Fear is a spirt from the devil. The bible tells in 2 Timothy 2: 7 "For God has not given us a spirit of fear, but of power and of love and of a sound mind." So when we feel fearful, we must recognize the source. It is not from God. Fear and faith cannot live together. When you meditate on the word of God and understand the power that is within you is greater than any obstacle that may confront you, then fear will have no room in you.

So based on this understanding, is there any goal too big for you to accomplish? Is there any person that is too intimidating? Is there any opposition you can't win? Is there an educational level you can't achieve? Is there a speech you can't give? Is there a salary you cannot reach? Is there a position you can't get to? Is your color, gender, age, experience or your environment going to limit you? No! None of these things have the power to hold you back. Nothing, simply nothing, is impossible for you. There is greater power within you. You are unlimited because there is a limitless power within you.

Questions for personal reflection:

1. When do you feel inferior or insecure?

2. Have you ever wanted to do something big, but dropped the idea because it was too big? What was it?

3. Why did you think you were too small to accomplish it?

4. Have you ever declined a promotion or new responsibility because you thought someone else would be better for the job than you?

5. Synonyms of valor are "courage," "bravery," "fearless," "boldness," etc. Do you believe you have these traits? Why or why not?

6. How can you see yourself differently based on the chapter you just read?

Chapter Nine

Exit strategy from negative emotions

We all have days where we suddenly feel overwhelmed, frustrated, or helpless. Yesterday we may have thought we overcame the problem or that we were above the circumstance, but today we feel the weight of the hardship. When this happens, our mood changes and we retreat into the corner of self-pity. The enemy seems to be able to push just the right button, a weak and vulnerable spot, that suddenly changes our emotional state. So what do we do about it?

We need an exit strategy to help us overcome negative emotions such as fear, anxiety, stress, hopelessness, and uselessness, since they impede us from becoming all we can be. Every time someone in the Information Technology field deploys a new code, someone has to write step-by-step instructions to reverse the code back to its current functionality in case things do not go as planned. Likewise, a negative emotion that does not have an exit plan is like a cycle that feeds on itself with no end in sight. If you have not developed tools to get out of the cycle, you can keep spiraling downward in your negativity.

If this example is too technical for you, then imagine a fire drill, the purpose of which is to practice exiting a building in a reasonable time in case of an emergency. It is usually practiced on days when there is no emergency. Usually an alarm will sound and everyone exits hurriedly to the safe place. Then, if an emergency arises, everyone will automatically exit to the designated area just like they practiced during the drill. Potential emergency subverted.

Likewise, we need an exit plan when toxic emotions suddenly overwhelm us and we need to exit the undesired state of mind. While we're feeling emotionally strong (or while we're in a state of "non-emergency"), we need steps to practice that will kick in automatically to bring us out of the undesired state quickly.

The following steps and affirmations have helped me:

1. Knowing that God loves me

    I use the following affirmation statement: "My father loves me. He wants the best for me and all things will change for my benefit. I have everything I need."
    The scripture base for the affirmation statement is Romans 8:32 (NKJV): "He who did not spare His own Son, but delivered Him up for us all, how shall He not with Him also freely give us all things?"

2. Focusing on Jesus, not the problem

    Affirmation statement: "I will take my eyes off the people and the circumstance and look at Jesus."
    The scripture base for this affirmation statement is Acts 2:25 (NKJV): "I foresaw the Lord always before my face, For He is at my right hand, that I may not be shaken."

3. Commanding the situation to change.

    Affirmation statement: "Jesus has finished everything for me on the cross. I don't have to beg God. I just need to command the enemy to release what belongs to me."
    The scripture base for the affirmation statement is Luke 10:19 (NKJV): "Behold, I give you the authority to trample on serpents and scorpions, and over all the power of the enemy, and nothing shall by any means hurt you." Use these three steps or come up with your own that are applicable to your situation. The bottom line is our mind

70

needs a tool to deal with difficult situations. Having an exit plan will break the cycle of emotional rollercoaster rides.

Let us look this three-step exit strategy in detail.

God loves you

The anchor you will need to go back to many times in your life is knowing that God loves you. It is the foundation of our lives. A person who knows God loves him or her is unshakable. A person who doubts God's love is unstable and will be shaken by any wind of hardship. 1 John 4:8-10 (NKJV) confirms this:

> "He who does not love does not know God, for **God is love**. In this the love of God was manifested toward us, that God has sent His only begotten Son into the world, that we might live through Him. In this is love, not that we loved God, but that He loved us and sent His Son to be the propitiation for our sins.

God is love. Love is His identity. Our actions cannot increase or decrease His love. God manifested His love by sacrificing His Son Jesus so we may live through Him. It did not require that we love Him first. He loved us first. He loves us as much as He loves Jesus. How do we know that? The value of something is determined by how much you pay for it. If you buy a car, the amount you pay for it and the value of the car are equal. God paid His only Son to redeem us. We are *that* valuable to Him. He loves us both through His word and through His actions every day of our lives.

Our enemy, the devil, does not want us to understand God's love. In fact, he brings many hardships and trials to cause us to question God's love. This is why God assures us several times in the Bible that He loves us. God's love is giving, generous, sacrificial, and unchangeable.

In Matthew 7:11 (NKJV), "If you then, being evil, know how to give good gifts to your children, how much more will your Father who is in heaven give good things to those who ask Him!" Jesus seemed puzzled about how people think of His Father. Even an evil person gives good gifts to his or her own children. So why wouldn't God, who is love, give good things to His children?

Unfortunately, the enemy has twisted our thinking so much that we do not even believe we deserve good things; therefore, we do not ask for them. Romans 8:32 (NKJV) says, however, "He who did not spare His own Son, but delivered Him up for us all, how shall He not with Him also freely give us all things?" So if God did not spare His own Son to redeem us, why would He withhold healing, a spouse, children, prosperity, satisfaction in life, and maximized potential?

God is love and love is God. In 1 Corinthians 13:4-7 (NKJV) below, I replaced the word "love" with "God" so you can see how He manifests His love toward you.

> [God] is patient, [God] is kind. [God] does not envy, [God] does not boast, [God] is not proud. [God] does not dishonor others, [God] is not self-seeking, [God] is not easily angered, [God] keeps no record of wrongs. [God] does not delight in evil but rejoices with the truth. [God] always protects, always trusts, always hopes, always perseveres.

God loves you so much that He is all these things and more for you. When you feel that nobody is watching out for you, that everyone is running after his or her own interests and forsaking you, that people are taking advantage of you, that no one appreciates your efforts, or that someone is committing an injustice against you, you have a weapon you can fight these emotions with. Tell the enemy:

> No. God loves me. My future is bright. I will not fail. I will not be anxious or stressed because everything will

change for my benefit. If no human will stand on my behalf, God will stand on my behalf.

When the enemy shows you a dark future, failure, anxiety, mountains of debt, or a ruined reputation, meditating on God's love will help you exit that dark future that the enemy has put in your mind to deceive you. Knowing God loves you and knowing God wants the best for you will set you free from trapping emotions.

Questions for personal reflection:

1. Why do you think people have a difficult time believing God loves them unconditionally?

2. Why do you think God loves you?

3. Is there something you can do to increase His love?

4. What can you do to remind yourself that God loves you when you struggle with negative emotions?

5. Meditate on God's love until your mind is completely convinced that God loves you.

Look at Jesus, not at the problem

When negative emotions begin to arise, that means your focus is not on Jesus. If you start seeing a problem as unsolvable, impossible, or bigger than your ability, it means that somewhere you have started focusing on the issue instead of Jesus Christ. This is the lesson that Jesus taught Peter in Matthew 14:28-31 (NKJV):

> "And Peter answered Him and said, "Lord, if it is You, command me to come to You on the water." So He said, "Come." And when Peter had come down out of the boat, he walked on the water to go to Jesus. But when he saw that the wind was boisterous, he was afraid; and beginning to sink he cried out, saying, "Lord, save me!" And immediately Jesus stretched out His hand and caught him, and said to him, "O you of little faith, why did you doubt?""

Peter was full of faith when he stepped off the boat. He believed if Jesus commanded him to do so, he would be able to walk on water just like He did. But the moment Peter shifted his focus from Jesus to the wind, he became afraid and started sinking.

When we focus on a situation that is challenging us rather than Christ, it has a tendency to seem bigger than our God. If you do not want to sink into a negative emotional spiral, then focus on Christ. Think of how much bigger your God is than the situation. Remember your positon in Christ and imagine yourself above the situation and the circumstances. Problems and hardships are not on top of us. We are above them and they are under our feet. Ephesians 2:5-6 (NKJV) tells us we are seated with Christ in the heavenly places.

"Even when we were dead in trespasses, made us alive together with Christ (by grace you have been saved), and raised us up together, and made us sit together in the heavenly places in Christ Jesus."

You might ask yourself, "How am I seated with Christ when I am physically in this world?" This is not about your physical position, but about your spiritual position.

Spiritually, we were dead because of our trespasses. But now, through Christ, we are alive, raised up, and seated together in the heavenly places in Christ Jesus. When you get overwhelmed, remember your positon in Christ and show the enemy who is in charge. When you realize you have dominion over the situation, you will be able to exit the negativity.

Questions for personal reflection:

1. Pick one issue/problem/hardship you are dealing with. Do you feel you are in charge, or do you feel it is overwhelming you?

2. If it is overwhelming you, how can you reverse this position?

3. Where is your spiritual position in Christ?

4. Do you tend to want people to do something for you, and become disappointed when they don't do what you want? Do you compare yourself with others and feel bad about yourself? If the answer to either of these questions is "yes," then your focus is in the wrong place.

5. How can you stop focusing on people?

Command and confess to change the situation

Jesus told the disciples in Mark 4:35 (NKJV), "...Let us cross over to the other side." They did not attempt to cross over by their own will. They listened to the Lord's word and set out to do what Jesus commanded them. They assumed it would be a smooth ride. They were planning to sail with no issues. Mark 4:37 (NKJV) says, however, "And a great windstorm arose and the waves beat into the boat, so that it was already filling." This was not smooth sailing. It was going to be tough.

The first lesson here is that doing the will of God does not guarantee a smooth ride. When the disciples encountered the storm amidst a sleeping Jesus, they could have responded in many ways, but they chose a response that did not please Jesus.

The disciples could have:

1. Aborted the sinking ship and jumped into the water to try to save themselves by swimming to shore. This would have not been a good response. They could have all drowned. Besides, it would have never gotten the disciples to their destination. Even if they had survived the swim, the current could have taken them in any direction instead of the one God had intended for them. Unfortunately many people opt to abort a situation when the going gets tough. This is especially true for situations that carry big consequences such as difficulties with school, jobs, marriage, etc.
2. Used a bucket to try to keep the water out of the boat. This choice would have led to exhaustion and restlessness since it would have been impossible to keep the water from overfilling the boat. Manmade efforts that do not include God's will are futile. They only keep us busy while providing no destination; they keep us working all the time without producing any fruit. If we don't deal with the root

cause of the problem, the symptom will just keep coming. So this response would not have solved the problem.

3. Awakened Jesus.

The disciples had enough sense not to choose the first two responses. They decided to wake Jesus up, but they accused Him of not caring about them. We respond to God the same way after He has instructed us to do something in the midst of a situation that's not smooth or the way we want it. We ask Jesus questions such as, "Don't you see this injustice?" "Don't you hear my prayer?" "Don't you care what happens to me?" "How can you let this happen?" "Why? Why? Why?"

The disciples' response did not please Jesus. So in Mark 4:40 (NKJV) "...He said to them, 'Why are you so fearful? How is it that you have no faith?'

Prayers that are full of complaints indicate we don't know the full capacity of our God and we are not mature in our spiritual growth.

4. Commanded the wind.

This choice would have pleased Jesus. First, it would have shown the disciples trusted Jesus to accomplish what He had promised. Second, choosing to rebuke the enemy that had come to abort their God-given vision would have shown they knew their authority in Christ. When you encounter the storms of life, command them as Jesus commanded the wind to quell the storm in Mark 4:39-41 (NKJV): "Then He arose and rebuked the wind, and said to the sea, 'Peace, be still!' And the wind ceased and there was a great calm."

We all face choices when we encounter hardships in life. How would you like to respond, going forward?

Confess positive affirmation words

In addition to commanding the situation to change, confessing the word of God aloud is also an important spiritual exercise. Our mind needs to be transformed by the word of God since we have accepted many untrue things about ourselves based on our upbringing, our culture, our education, our experiences, or our religion. We lead our minds out of negative emotions using our mouths. Proverbs 18:21 (NKJV) says, "Death and life are in the power of the tongue, And those who love it will eat its fruit."

Speaking positive statements over your life will produce the fruits of success: prosperity, joy, perseverance, consistency, victory, and so on. But repeatedly speaking failure and beating yourself up with condemnation will only reap those things in your life. Jesus said *in Mark 11:23* (NKJV), "For assuredly, I say to you, whoever says to this mountain, 'Be removed and be cast into the sea,' and does not doubt in his heart, but believes that those things he says will be done, he will have whatever he says."

Notice that Jesus said the word, "say" four times in this verse, showing us that "saying" is very important. There are a lot of mountains standing before us—mountains of debt, education, business, or family problems. Jesus says, however, they can be removed and thrown into the sea. All you need to do is speak to your mountain, do not doubt what you say, believe it is done, and then you will have possession over it. Notice you believe first and then you possess it.

I have written some affirmation prayers to get you started confessing the Word of God.

Confessions of Identity

John 1:12-13 (NKJV): "But as many as received Him, to them He gave the right to become children of God, to those who believe in His name: who were born, not of blood, nor of the will of the flesh, nor of the will of man, but of God."

1. I have received Jesus Christ as my Lord and Savior. I am a child of God. I am part of God's family. God is my father and I am His child.

Genesis 1:26 (NKJV): "Then God said, 'Let Us make man in Our image, according to Our likeness; let them have dominion over the fish of the sea, over the birds of the air, and over the cattle, over all the earth and over every creeping thing that creeps on the earth.'"

2. God created me in His image and in His likeness. That means I look like Him in my physical appearance, so I will not speak anything negative about it because everything He created is good. Being created in His likeness also means I have the same character and behavior. So from now on I see as He sees, I think as He thinks, I speak as He speaks, and I act as He acts.
    God create me to have dominion in this world. He created me to be a leader. That means I influence my family, church, work, community and the world in a positive way.

Romans 8:19-39 (NIV): "For the creation waits in eager expectation for the children of God to be revealed."

3. Creation waits for me to bring a solution to its problem. Creation waits for me to be a light in this world. Creation waits for me to be a positive influence.

Jeremiah 29:11 (NIV): "For I know the plans I have for you," declares the Lord, "plans to prosper you and not to harm you, plans to give you hope and a future."

4. God has a plan for my life. I have a hope and a great future. His plan is to prosper me and not to harm me. I prosper when I solve problems. He created me to bring solutions. I am a problem solver.

Matthew 5:16 (NKJV): "Let your light so shine before men, that they may see your good works and glorify your Father in heaven."

5. God created me to be a light in the darkness. I will not hide. I will not fear. I will not disqualify myself. A light cannot be hidden. I will do the good works and my Father in heaven will be glorified.

Romans 8:32 (NKJV): "He who did not spare His own Son, but delivered Him up for us all, how shall He not with Him also freely give us all things?"

6. God is not angry with me. God loves me unconditionally. His thoughts toward me are always good. He is a good Father. If He did not spare His own Son so I can be reconciled with Him, He will hold no other thing back from me. He will not hold back healing; He will not hold back prosperity; and He has given me everything I need for life and Godliness.

1 Corinthians 15:10 (NKJV): "But by the grace of God I am what I am, and His grace toward me was not in vain; but I labored more abundantly than they all, yet not I, but the grace of God which was with me."

7. I am what I am by the grace of God. All the success I have and will have is by the grace of God. I accept God's grace to live a life that is effective and fruitful. I receive God's grace to do all the good works that I am passionate about. The grace of God will help me accomplish even more than I dream or think.

1 Peter 2:9 (NKJV): "But you are a chosen generation, a royal priesthood, a holy nation, His own special people, that you may proclaim the praises of Him who called you out of darkness into His marvelous light;"

8. I am a chosen generation for such a time as this to proclaim God's goodness to all. I am a royal priesthood to proclaim to others that they have been reconciled with God. I am part of the holy nation, which is the body of Christ. I am one of His own special people. I am valuable. I have something good to offer to those who are in the darkness.

2 Timothy 1:7 (NKJV): "For God has not given us a spirit of fear, but of power and of love and of a sound mind."

9. God did not give me a spirit of fear. I reject the spirit of fear in Jesus' name. I have been given power: power over the enemy, power to change circumstances, power to be all God created me to be. I have been given love, to love others as God has loved me. I have a sound mind. My mind thinks clearly according to the word of God. My mind is sound, sharp, intelligent, and wise. No more limitations. No more inferiority. No more hesitations.

Hebrews 4:11 (NKJV): "Let us therefore be diligent to enter that rest, lest anyone fall according to the same example of disobedience."

10. I enter the rest through the finished work of Jesus Christ. I will not labor to become righteous because I have become righteous through Christ. I will not labor for God to love me and accept me since He has already done so. Whatever I do, I start from the finished work of Christ. I start with rest. No more stress. I receive the supply of His grace to do my assignment in this world.

Proverbs 22:29 (NKJV): "Do you see a man who excels in his work? He will stand before kings; He will not stand before unknown men."

11. The talents, skills, and gifts I have come from God. When I utilize them, God will multiply them to benefit multitudes of people as He multiplied the five fish and two loaves and fed 5,000 people. The gifts I have will take me to high places and positions.

Questions for personal reflection:

1. What choices do you have when you encounter hardships?

2. Why do you think it pleases God when we command a situation to change?

3. Why is confessing affirmative words important?

4. Create a list of scriptures and affirmative words that are relevant for you.

CREATION IS WAITING FOR YOU!

Chapter Ten

The Holy Spirit will help you

The Holy Spirit is the most ignored topic in Christianity although the Holy Spirit is equal to the Father and the Son.

Matthew 28:19 (NKJV) "Go therefore and make disciples of all the nations, baptizing them in the name of the Father and of the Son and of the Holy Spirit."

We cannot live the Christian life successfully without the knowledge of the Holy Spirit. It is so important that Jesus told the disciples that it is to our advantage Jesus goes to the Father so He can send us the Holy Spirit. (John 16:7-11). The bible defines the Holy Spirit as many things: our helper, teacher, reminder of Jesus's word (John 14:26), our intercessor (Romans 8:26), truth (1 John 5:6), giver of life (Romans 8:11), speaker and guide (John 16:13), and so much more. He comes to live in us when we accept Christ as our Savior. We receive his power when we get baptized and manifest it by speaking in tongues.

Before Jesus ascended to heaven, He told the disciples to stay in Jerusalem so they can receive power. (Act 1:8) The bible tells us that on the day of Pentecost, "..they were all filled with the Holy Spirit and began to speak with other tongues, as the Spirit gave them utterance." Jesus said those who believe in him will have the following signs follow them:

Mark 16:17-18 (NKJV) " And these signs will follow those who believe: In My name they will cast out demons; they will speak with new tongues; they will take up serpents; and if they drink anything deadly, it will by no means hurt them; they will lay hands on the sick, and they will recover."

Speaking in a "new tongue" is a sign that you are baptized with the Holy Spirit. Speaking in tongues (also known as praying in the Spirit), is a heavenly language given to children of God. When praying in tongue you are edifying yourself (1 Corinthians 14:4), building up yourself (Jude 20), speaking mysteries (1 Corinthians 14:2) and praying the will of God (Romans 8: 26-28).

However, with all the benefit the Holy Spirit brings to our life, why do we underutilize Him? It requires faith to believe in the Holy Spirit and an understanding that He is not the wind or a dove as he is sometimes pictured, but a Spirit that is given to us to empower us. When we speak in tongues, we do not understand what we are saying, and I think this is why we do not pray in tongues as much as we should. But when we do by faith, we will find inner strength, the word of God will become alive in us, and we become calmer and bolder.

The other reason I believe we do not acknowledge the Holy Spirit, is because of our erroneous understanding of why the Holy Spirit came. I think we confuse condemnation and conviction. We know the Holy Spirt came to convict us but we are not clear on what He is convicting us about. The bible tells us the Holy Spirit came to do three things: He came to convict the world of sin, righteousness and judgment.

John 16:8-11 (NKJV)

"And when He has come, He will convict the world of sin, and of righteousness, and of judgment: of sin, because they do not believe in Me; of righteousness, because I go to My Father and you see Me no more; of judgment, because the ruler of this world is judged."

The bible verse above further explains he came to convict the world of sin. This is one sin and not multiple sins. It is for non-Christians because they did not believe in Jesus Christ. In other words, the unbelievers get convicted because they do not believe that Jesus came to tell them they are reconciled with

God. For those who are Christians, the Holy Spirit convicts us about our righteousness. He tells us repeatedly we are righteous in Christ. This is supported by another scripture in 1Corinthians 2:12 (NKJV) "Now we have received, not the spirit of the world, but the Spirit who is from God, that we might know the things that have been freely given to us by God." The Holy Spirit continually helps us know what has been given to us freely such as righteousness, freedom from bondages, healing, prosperity, etc. The Holy Spirit is not the one who says to us, "You failed again. You are just useless". Thirdly, the Holy Spirit came to remind us the devil has been judged and Jesus has triumphed over him. When there is wrong or conflicting information in our mind about the Holy Spirit, it pulls us back to the familiar, which is walking without any supernatural power.

In addition to speaking in tongues for personal edification, there are other supernatural spiritual gifts such as; word of wisdom, word of knowledge, faith, healing, working miracles, prophecy, discerning of spirits, tongues (tongues that can be interpreted to understandable language. It is different than the one used for personal edification) and interpretation of tongues. 1 Corinthians 12:8-11

These gifts are given to benefit the church, the body of Christ, and they do manifest in some churches. We must remember that these are gifts from God. It does not mean the person who has these gifts is super spiritual or has better characters. They are given by the grace of God and they get sharper as the person grows in the word of God and in character. These gifts should never say anything contrary to God's word and that is why we need to know the word of God so we can discern the accuracy of these gifts.

How do you get baptized in the Holy Spirit and get these supernatural gifts? You ask your father to give it to you.

Luke 11:13 (NKJV) "If you then, being evil, know how to give good gifts to your children, how much more will your heavenly Father give the Holy Spirit to those who ask Him!"

Once you understand who the Holy Spirit is, then pray for the father to baptize you. You can also ask other Christians to pray for you as well. Once you have the new language, train yourself to pray daily, reminding you all its benefits. The generation who fellowships with the Holy Spirit and taps into this power along with a balanced understanding of the word of God will be the catalyst for change.

Questions for personal reflection:

1. Who is the Holy Spirit?

2. What is the sign of being baptized with Holy Spirit?

3. What are the benefits of speaking in tongues?

4. What is the Holy Spirit convicting you about?

5. How can you remind yourself to make speaking in tongues and fellowshipping with Holy Spirit your daily practice?

CREATION IS WAITING FOR YOU!

Part III

Questions from the youth

CREATION IS WAITING FOR YOU!

Questions from the youth

As part of my research, I interviewed a few young people to get their feedback about the topics I raised in this book. They believe encouraging the youth to serve the Lord in a way that helps solve the problems of their generation is important. They did raise some questions, however, which I address in the following pages.

1. **"Why should I care about contributing to creation?"**

   This is a key question that must be addressed. The question is also implicitly asking, "Why should anyone go the extra mile? Why not live a mediocre life? Why add the extra effort?"

   First, it is not part of your nature to be ordinary and to live a mediocre life. Within the depths of all human hearts is a longing to give back, to make a positive impact, and to change the world. God did not create you to be insignificant. He had a specific purpose and design when He formed you, even before you were in your mother's womb. God created you in His image and character so you can reflect this image and character in the way you think, talk, walk, and act like God. You are not God, but you are a child of God. A child inherits the DNA, character, and behavior of His Father; therefore, you have the potential to be loving, compassionate, giving, optimistic, and transformative—all the characteristics we attribute to God. Your imagination needs to be as big as God's. You are not ordinary, but extraordinary. You are not only natural; you are supernatural. You are created to be a solution to the world!

Questions such as "Why me?" are caused by thinking, "I am nobody"; "I have nothing good to contribute, so I just want to live a mediocre life"; and "There are too many problems in this world that are too impossible to solve." The chapter, "Overcome Inferiority and Insecurity" explains that these types of self-defeating thoughts are not from God, so please re-read that chapter.

See yourself as God sees you. God sees you as an individual of "mighty valor," a champion, and a game changer because nothing is impossible for the God who created you, who formed you in His image and likeness, and who lives inside you, if you truly believe. So believe in His ability to ignite passion in your heart. Mark 9:23 (NKJV) says, "Jesus said to him, 'If you can believe, all things are possible to him who believes.'" Replace every thought you have that says "I can't"; "It is impossible"; or "I will fail" with Philippians 4:13 (NKJV): "I can do all things through Christ who strengthens me."

And finally, many who think this way may just want to live for themselves. They say things like, "I do not care about anybody else"; "I will consume what I produce and not leave anything to anybody"; "It is a cruel world out here and I have to watch out for myself." I feel sorry for these people because the enemy has deceived them and they believe this is the way to survive. The enemy has cheated them out of many great experiences and out of leaving a mark on the world.

Some young people have this attitude because they've had bad experiences in the past. No matter the reason, it is still wrong thinking. People who say these things do not fully trust God. They do not believe God will provide, so they choose not to share what they have, such as their money or time. They also don't trust God to protect them, so they don't come out of their comfort zones. Every decision they make is based on whether or not it will benefit them. As a result, they do not even have good interpersonal relationships.

The good news is, it is not too late to change! God is very gracious. He does not need years to do something dynamic with your life. The moment you realize you have the wrong perspective, you can renew your mind and start anew.

2. "Can I fulfill my duty by donating money?"

Many people contribute to the well-being of creation by donating money. Wealth can transform society. You can support an organization financially if you believe in the vision. Those called to be kingdom of God financiers are blessings to many visionaries. Donating money is wonderful but God also wants us to use our unique gifts and talents to further His Kingdom.

3. "Talking about having confidence and knowing my identity is great, but how do I actually get these qualities? The youth of today are already hurting and bleeding spiritually; how can they overcome their situation?"

A 15-year-old-girl asked me this question, using the hurting and bleeding analogy. Her point was that today's youth already have issues with their confidence and identity. They are hurting and do not know how to resolve them. Everyone else is telling them to fix their problems, but they do not have the tools.

This question reminds me of the story of the Good Samaritan in Luke 10:30-35 (NKJV) that tells us about a man who was wounded by thieves and abandoned by passersby:

> "Then Jesus answered and said: "A certain man went down from Jerusalem to Jericho, and fell among thieves, who stripped him of his clothing,

wounded him, and departed, leaving him half dead. Now by chance a certain priest came down that road. And when he saw him, he passed by on the other side. Likewise a Levite, when he arrived at the place, came and looked, and passed by on the other side. But a certain Samaritan, as he journeyed, came where he was. And when he saw him, he had compassion. So he went to him and bandaged his wounds, pouring on oil and wine; and he set him on his own animal, brought him to an inn, and took care of him. On the next day, when he departed, he took out two denarii, gave them to the innkeeper, and said to him, 'Take care of him; and whatever more you spend, when I come again, I will repay you.'"

The enemy has also deceived many of today's young people into thinking God has abandoned them. Just like the man traveling to Jericho, the enemy has stolen their innocence, stripped off their dignity, wounded them, and left them physically and emotionally half-dead. Unfortunately, just as the religious people passing by pretended not to see the wounded man in the story, some Christians have ignored and abandoned the youth who have made mistakes. How should our society approach the many wounded young women and men who have been led astray for different reasons?

1. With Compassion

Today's youth have more challenges, temptations, and distractions than any other generation. They do not need to travel far to find trouble because modern technology has given them access to everything. While there are a lot of benefits to such technology, the enemy is also using it to distract the youth from the good they can do in the world. 1 Peter 5:8 (NKJV) says: "Be sober, be vigilant; because your adversary the devil walks about like a roaring lion, seeking whom he may devour."

The enemy tries to devour young people's potential and innocence with every opportunity he finds. He knows if he traps young people with distractions, he will destroy their future and potential, so he works extra hard to do so. Responding to young people with a judgmental attitude will only push them further away. Compassion is the key because Jesus has a compassionate heart toward youth. As leaders, parents, and teachers of young people, we must reflect that same heart of God. Like the Good Samaritan, we must have compassion toward those who are hurt.

2. Teaching Them About the Love of God

The Samaritan poured on oil and wine after bandaging the wounds of the man who was robbed. Oil helps advance the healing process and wine helps purify and disinfect the wound. I can't think of a better palliative to help a wounded young person heal than teaching him or her about God's love and demonstrating that love in action. Our youth need many doses of God's love to heal. A young individual who loves the world's sinful behavior does not understand the Father's love for him or her. 1 John 2:15 (NKJV) says, "Do not love the world or the things in the world. If anyone loves the world, the love of the Father is not in him."

When our youth understand the unconditional love of God, they are less likely to fall prey to the temptations of the world. Love motivates change. In my role as a Sunday school teacher, I found myself using the Word of God to purge all the lies the enemy told the youth about themselves because they were believing so many untrue things. The media, school, parents, and peers may tell young people they are "useless," "unwanted," "dumb," "ugly," or "good for nothing," but youth leaders need to remind those in their groups of who they are in

Christ and work to replace all the negative thoughts and ideas others have spoken to them with the positive Word of God.

3. Caring for them

Wounds get bandaged to protect the sores from foreign elements and keep the healing medicine inside. Youth need dedicated people who will care for them until they are completely healed. Serving the younger generation is a difficult task. It requires time; patience; and resilience; physically, spiritually, and emotionally. Today's wounded youth need time to heal. Churches needs to give a high priority to this ministry so that young people will have a place of refuge—a facility that will empower, train, and equip them before they set out to impact the world.

Now that we have talked about what the church, parents, and community should do for hurting youth, what should the youth do for themselves?

Younger generations have an important role to play in their own restoration. Using the Good Samaritan passage as context, young people need to trust Jesus—to realize He is not like the Priest or the Levite who abandoned the robbed man. The Priest went out of his way to avoid the poor man by walking to the other side of the road. The Levite looked at the man but walked away, as well.

Hebrews 2:17, however, says that Jesus is our High Priest, who bought atonement for all the sins of humanity. When Father God sees you, He does not see all your weaknesses. He does not wiggle and point His finger and accuse you. Instead He sees that all your sins and mistakes have been paid by Jesus the High Priest and He sees you as righteous, acceptable, forgiven, and loved. Like the Good Samaritan, He will never abandon you (Hebrew 13:5).

The starting point for being more self-confident and having a stronger identity is to understand how God sees you. Replace

CREATION IS WAITING FOR YOU!

the image you may have of an angry, hard-to-please, distant, judgmental, and cruel God with an image of a God who is merciful, loving, closer than your breath, encouraging, kind, and always pleased by His children.

The next step is to change how you think about yourself. Replace every pessimistic or fearful thought you have about yourself that says you are lazy, stupid, incompetent, shy, mediocre, unworthy, self-conscious, sensitive, angry, or poor, with positive, image-boosting thoughts. For each negative thought, replace it with its opposite. Find a verse in the Bible that will affirm the positive thought you want to keep. After you have found a verse, meditate on it. Your mind can only be changed by the repetition of positive thoughts.

Your negative thoughts took root after many years of hearing other people say negative things about you. While some were verbal, others were subliminal. To flush out these negative voices, you will need to renew your mind, as the Bible instructs us to do in Romans 12:2 (NKJV): "And do not be conformed to this world, but be transformed by the renewing of your mind, that you may prove what is that good and acceptable and perfect will of God."

Be conscious of your thoughts. When you catch yourself thinking things that do not line up with God's word, replace them with thoughts that do. This is what it means to not conform to the world and be transformed into who you are in Christ. Worldly thoughts are not just the obvious things such as stealing, lying, or adultery; they also include fear and anxiety. When these types of thoughts are removed, you will see your confidence rising. For more help, re-read the chapter titled, "Exit Strategy from the Negative Emotions."

4. "Can I make a difference while incarcerated?"

I have visited prisons a few times with other ministers. While it is heart wrenching to see human beings caged like animals, anyone anywhere can become a solution to the world. Although I do not personally understand the oppression felt by those who are imprisoned, the Bible gives us guidelines on how to overcome every type of situation. Paul was in jail quite a few times. In fact, in Acts 16:22-26 (NKJV), Paul and Silas were imprisoned for setting a slave girl free, who was possessed with a spirit of divination:

"Then the multitude rose up together against them; and the magistrates tore off their clothes and commanded them to be beaten with rods. And when they had laid many stripes on them, they threw them into prison, commanding the jailer to keep them securely. Having received such a charge, he put them into the inner prison and fastened their feet in the stocks.

But at midnight Paul and Silas were praying and singing hymns to God, and the prisoners were listening to them. Suddenly there was a great earthquake, so that the foundations of the prison were shaken; and immediately all the doors were opened and everyone's chains were loosed."

Paul and Silas' experience was inhumane—they were beaten like animals and restrained from moving. They could have become bitter with God and angry with everyone, but as usual, they were praying and singing hymns to God in the midst of this dire circumstance. God, pleased with their response, caused an earthquake to loosen their chains. We can learn so much from this story.

First, realize you can be physically incarcerated but spiritually free. You may have been imprisoned by your own wrongdoing or you may have been wrongly accused. In order for you to be a solution to the problems in creation, the change needs to start with you. This change happens first at the spiritual level. God may not free you from jail with an earthquake like He freed Paul, but He can certainly free you from spiritual and mental imprisonment.

Being spiritually free means being forgiven. There is no more condemnation when you genuinely repent. The moment you invite Christ to be your Lord and Savior, you are spiritually free. Paul and Silas were in prison, but their spirits were free and they were able to communicate with God by praying and singing. The beauty of being a Christian is that when you accept Christ, you start with a clean slate. Jesus Christ was crucified on the cross for your sins to make you righteous with God. It is a substitution. He took all our sins and we took His righteousness.

2 Corinthians 5:21 (NKJV) says, "For He made Him who knew no sin to be sin for us, that we might become the righteousness of God in Him." Because God made you righteous, there is no need to define yourself as a sinner. You were a sinner *before* you knew Christ. The new person you have become in Christ is righteous. The old person has died with Christ and the new you have been raised with Christ. 2 Corinthians 5:17 (NKJV) says, "Therefore, if anyone is in Christ, he is a new creation; old things have passed away; behold, all things have become new."

The old person who had a tendency to steal, cheat, curse, fight, or struggle with addiction is gone. This is not your identity anymore. The enemy may bring your past back to memory and try to condemn you with accusation. Know that this is a lie. He is simply trying to keep you from living a life of freedom. The enemy wants you to beat yourself up and live in misery for the rest of your life. As I wrote in the chapter titled, "God is Not Angry with you," there is no condemnation once you are in Christ.

You may wonder why you are still tempted to do wrong, even though you have accepted Christ. Understand the person who wants to do bad things is not you. That person has died with Christ. The real you, is righteous. You may have lingering bad habits and vices, but these can be broken by repeatedly reminding yourself of who you are in

Christ. Spiritual change occurs immediately, but your mental transformation takes time.

Romans 12:2 (NKJV) says, "And do not be conformed to this world, but be transformed by the renewing of your mind, that you may prove what is that good and acceptable and perfect will of God." So work to transform your mind by focusing on your new identity in Christ. Affirm you are not a sinner, but righteous. You are not rejected, but loved. Re-read the chapter in this book called "Exit Strategy from the Negative Emotions."

If you are imprisoned, another challenge to your mental state is your sense of value as a human being. When your basic right to freedom has been taken from you, when you are treated inhumanely, when others around you act brutally toward you, or when you feel disrespected in your environment, the enemy can chip away at your dignity. Even though justice must be served for the laws of the country you trespassed, this level of punishment is still emotionally difficult.

The good news is that you can overcome this. People or circumstances do not give you your value. God does. God has created you in His image and likeness. He was not ashamed to create you like Himself. He valued you so much that in order to reunite you to Himself, He decided your value was equal to that of His son, Jesus.

You are very valuable to God, even though the world may send you the message that you are not. Continually work to fight such devaluating messages and remind yourself of your true worth. You may not have education or money, but those things do not define you. You can lift your head up and be confident that you are most valued to God. Material possessions, status, and fame in this world are temporary. Put your focus on things above, which are eternal. Colossians 3:1-3 (NKJV) says:

"If then you were raised with Christ, seek those things which are above, where Christ is, sitting at the right hand of God. Set your mind on things above, not on things on the earth. For you died, and your life is hidden with Christ in God."

Second, understand your spiritual freedom can influence your physical experience. Regardless of your circumstances, you can live in peace, contentment, joy, forgiveness and manifest all the other fruits of the Spirit in your life. Galatians 5:22-23 (NKJV) tells us what these fruits are: "But the fruit of the Spirit is love, joy, peace, longsuffering, kindness, goodness, faithfulness, gentleness, self-control. Against such there is no law."

When you change spiritually, people around you will be attracted to this change. You will be able to share the love of Jesus, who gave you a new lease on life. Even in prison, you can be a solution. You can be a light for those who are in spiritual and mental darkness. You can also influence people around you in a positive way. Did you know that Paul wrote most of his epistles while he was in prison? These Holy Spirit-inspired letters from two thousand years ago still impact us today! You are unlimited, even in prison. You can be a solution to creation wherever you are, regardless of your circumstances.

5. **"How can a youth in a developing country, who lacks many basic needs, bring a solution to creation?"**

Not all young people in developing countries struggle with getting their basic needs met, though the majority grow up witnessing lack, limited opportunities, and extremely poor living circumstances. Now, more than any other time in world history, creation in developing countries is waiting for its youth to bring solutions to these problems. Let us look at the following facts from an article in the BBC titled,

[1]"Head-to-head: Is Africa's young population a risk or an asset?":

- Africa has more people under age 20 than anywhere in the world and the continent's population is set to double to two billion by 2050.
- People aged 15-29 will continue to constitute about half the population of most countries in the Sub-Saharan region for the next three to five decades.
- Currently, the estimated median age in Sub-Saharan Africa is under 19.
- According to the CIA's website, [3]Ethiopian youth under age 25 comprise 65% of the country's 90 million people.

The BBC article also states, "There is a strong case to be made that a young population, or a poorly managed young population, leads to instability and civil conflict." This is true. The youth have become an easy target for brainwashing from those who practice extreme ideologies and religion; they have been lured into becoming child soldiers, terrorists, and victims of human trafficking. Leaders in developing countries are responsible for coming up with a policy that will help the youth become productive citizens.

As a spiritual youth leader, I know the unlocked potential of young people in developing countries can produce solutions to problems in creation. Africa may have many problems, but it has a large percentage of youth who can produce solutions to those problems. In order to stop unrest and conflict, the youth in developing nations will need spiritual and mental enlightenment.

Spiritual Enlightenment

Spiritual enlightenment starts by knowing who God is for you and who you are in Christ. How you define yourself or how you define God should not be based on your environment or current situation. Refuse to be a byproduct of a poor environment. The spiritual principles mentioned in this book are relevant for all and, as a reminder, convey the following messages:

1. You are created to be a solution.
2. You are created to be a light.
3. You are created to be a leader.
4. God is not angry with you.
5. Depend on God's grace.
6. Be a doer.
7. You can overcome fear, inferiority and insecurity.
8. You can develop an exit strategy from negative emotions by focusing on God's love; looking at Jesus, not at the problem; as well as commanding and confessing the situation to change.
9. Holy Spirit is within you to help

When you understand these spiritual principles, you will start to think as a victor rather than a victim. An individual with a victim mindset is someone who does not take responsibility for his or her destiny. This person is someone who waits for someone else to change his or her destiny but then becomes disappointed when it does not happen. John 5: 1-9 (NKJV) tells us about a man who was paralyzed for 38 years who went to the pool so he can be healed. In those days, if an angel of Lord came by and stirred the water, the first person who entered the pool would be healed. In this story, Jesus asked this man in verse 6, "Do you want to be well?" The story continues with:

> The sick man answered, "Sir, there is no one to help me get into the pool when the water starts moving. While I am coming to the water, someone else always gets in before me." Then Jesus said, "Stand up. Pick up your mat and walk." And immediately

the man was well; he picked up his mat and began to walk.

Picture this paralyzed man talking to Jesus, our Jehovah Rapha (the one who heals), who has all the power to heal him, complaining about how he does not have anyone to help him get into the pool to be healed! This man was not only paralyzed physically; he was paralyzed mentally, as well. Jesus asked him, "Do you want to get well?" not "Why you are not healed?" Unfortunately, we all act like this sometimes. Instead of looking to Jesus for our solution, we talk about how we do not have money, connections, or resources. But if we look to Jesus, He will set us free, spiritually and physically. Then we can become solutions to the world.

Mental Enlightenment

Our minds have incredible abilities, but how well they function is based on what they are fed and what they are exposed to. Ever heard of "thinking outside the box"? People who think *inside* the box base their decisions on what they see: limitations and impossibilities. They tend to be pessimistic. Those who think *outside* the box, on the other hand, are creative, think unconventionally, and do not have a vocabulary of impossibilities implanted in their consciousness. If plan A does not work, they move on to plan B.

Let us say, for example, that Mary wants to start a business, but she does not have the money. If Mary is an inside-the-box thinker, she is going to keep her mind from thinking creatively by saying, "I do not have money; therefore, I can't start a business." If her friend, Susan, thinks outside the box, however, she will come up with multiple scenarios on how to start a business, even with limited money. If one scenario does not work, she will try another. In her mind, the options are endless.

Proverbs 26:13-15 (NKJV) actually defines Mary's type of limited, inside-the-box thinking as laziness. A person who is lazy has a mind that is resigned and accepts the unacceptable situations of life:

> "The lazy man says, "There is a lion in the road!
> A fierce lion is in the streets!"
> As a door turns on its hinges,
> So does the lazy man on his bed.
> The lazy man buries his hand in the bowl;
> It wearies him to bring it back to his mouth."

It is interesting to observe what the lazy man in Proverbs is doing. He is still in his bed and thinks there is danger outside, yet he goes back to sleep. How does he even know there is a lion in the road? He does not even look outside to check, and because of his negative expectations, he chooses sleep instead of taking action. He is so lazy he will not even feed himself.

Many people have negative expectations because of the negative things they have seen or heard, so they have problems thinking outside the box. Instead of attempting to take action, they fold their hands in resignation based on potentially negative situations.

How do you train your mind to think outside the box? Here are six ways to boost your mental enlightenment:

1. **Formal Education**

   Academic knowledge is important and having a college-level education has become a competitive advantage. Yes, some people become successful even though they are not college educated, but the world has gotten much more competitive in the 21st century, and in order to compete, getting a formal education is a must. If you value yourself, education must become your priority so you can become valuable in the marketplace.

Unfortunately most formal education programs do not train you to become an entrepreneur. They prepare you to aspire to be an employee for a corporation. There is nothing wrong with being an employee and it a good starting point in your career. If you want to have greater influence and more freedom with your time, though, starting your own business is the way to do it. I highly recommend cultivating your entrepreneurial and innovative passions while gaining formal education.

2. **Informal Education**

Informal education, which is just as important as formal education, is the knowledge you gain outside a formal school environment. What you are exposed to is what helps you think outside the box. Expose yourself to new ways of thinking by reading books. I cannot emphasize this enough. Reading expands your thinking and helps you become a person with many ideas and not be shallow minded. Spend time reading the biographies of people who became successful. Books like these open your mind to new knowledge, add value to your perspective, and help you become financially independent. Traveling, meeting people from outside your circle, and cultivating a generally curious attitude will also help you gain a broader repertoire of knowledge.

3. **Wisdom**

Wisdom in Proverbs 2 is defined as a way to revere and fear God; a way to gain knowledge about God; a way to success; a way to be guarded and protected; and a way to discern what is right, just, and fair. It is important for the youth of today to gain wisdom so they can be a blessing to their families and nation. A lack of wisdom traps many young people in the wrong direction.

So how do you get wisdom? You seek it, you value it more than any possession, and you ask God for it. Proverbs 3:13-18 (NIV) says:

"Blessed are those who find wisdom,
    those who gain understanding,
for she is more profitable than silver
    and yields better returns than gold.
She is more precious than rubies;
    nothing you desire can compare with her.
Long life is in her right hand;
    in her left hand are riches and honor.
Her ways are pleasant ways,
    and all her paths are peace.
 She is a tree of life to those who take hold of her;
    those who hold her fast will be blessed."

When you have wisdom, you are able to turn the knowledge you have into a finished product. Many people have knowledge but do not apply it; therefore, they do not benefit from it. I have met brilliant people with many ideas that never came to realization because the people behind those ideas didn't have any wisdom. Proverbs 24:3-4 (NKJV) says:

"Through wisdom a house is built,
And by understanding it is established;
By knowledge the rooms are filled
With all precious and pleasant riches."

This scripture shows us it is wisdom that builds a house and it knowledge that will fill the room with good things. Understanding makes the house established. It will make it last, continue to exist, and pass it on to the next generation.

4. Skills Gained

You can gain many types of skills, such as technical, manufacturing, cosmetic, artistic, sales, linguistic, and many more by getting formal training or by volunteering to

help others. You should have multiple ways to generate income. Proverbs 10:4 (NKJV) says: "He who has a slack hand becomes poor,
But the hand of the diligent makes rich."
Use any idle time you have to increase your skills in different areas. If you are diligent, you will have the resources you need to bring solutions to the world by God's grace.

5. **Teamwork**
Organizing and working in teams is important to accomplishing any goal. A task that's difficult for one person will be easy with multiple people because each person can apply his or her strengths to the challenge. You can overcome any difficulty or hardship in front of you if you attack it in unity. Working in groups can resolve poverty, for example. You can start a business with a group or help group members accomplish a goal, one person at a time. Group collaboration fosters creativity and outside-the-box thinking, which creates solutions. Ecclesiastes 4:9-10 (NKJV) says:

> "Two are better than one,
> Because they have a good reward for their labor.
> For if they fall, one will lift up his companion.
> But woe to him who is alone when he falls,
> For he has no one to help him up."

Two are better than one, but more than two is even better. When people gather in unity with integrity, it creates a powerful team. As Christians, God designed us to work as a team. Each Christian is a member of the body of Christ, and the body of Christ is the universal church. We are designed as members of one body to work together with other members of that same body, as 1 Corinthians 12:12-14 (NKJV) says:

"For as the body is one and has many members, but all the members of that one body, being many, are one body, so also is Christ. For by one Spirit we were all baptized into one body—whether Jews or Greeks, whether slaves or free—and have all been made to drink into one Spirit. For in fact the body is not one member but many."

As you can see, we are all members of one body and we all need each other. One member is not more or less important than another. Each of us on God's team may have different functions but we all have equal value. When all members of the body of Christ work together in unity, we will reveal the full potential of God's power. The success of one member is the success of all and the suffering of one member is the suffering of all.

6. Mentors

A study[4] confirms that having mentors benefits people in the following ways:

- Increases high school graduation rates
- Lowers high school dropout rates
- Produces healthier relationships and lifestyle choices
- Produces better attitudes about school
- Produces higher college enrollment rates and higher educational aspirations
- Enhances self-esteem and self-confidence
- Improves behavior, both at home and at school
- Strengthens relationships with parents, teachers, and peers
- Improves interpersonal skills
- Decreases the likelihood of drug and alcohol use

Don't leave your personal development to chance or to the mercy of others. Take ownership and seek mentors who have accomplished more than you have. Shadowing someone with a wealth of experience you do not have opens your mind to new perspectives and new ways of being in the world. It is a fundamental way to broaden your horizons and develop outside-the-box thinking.

6. The book focuses mostly on those who are called to do non ministry works. What about those who are called to be full-time ministers?

Let's assume the percentage of full time ministers is 20%, (the actual percent may be a lot lower), there are still 80% of the youth who are not full time ministers. This is why this book focused on the non-ministerial group. But the content of this book is still very relevant to those who are called to full time ministry- it can help them understand the heart of God toward his people and encourage them to make the youth ministry a high priority in their churches. The youth are the next generation. If we invest in the youth now, then their future will be redeemed.

Jesus Christ commissioned all of us believers, to speak the good news of the reconciliation of God with the world and the world with God. In Mark 16:15 (NKJV) the Jesus says "...Go into all the world and preach the gospel to every creature." The way this message is delivered may not solely be from the pulpit but from any platform we are given, according to the sphere of influence we are called to impact, which can help point God's creatures to Christ. But that does not mean full time minsters are not needed.

Creation is waiting to hear the gospel of Jesus Christ and full time ministers are needed. In Romans 8:22 (NKJV) it states "For we know that the whole creation groans and labors with birth pangs together until now." The people of the world are groaning to hear the good news of the gospel. There are many people who are in darkness, who are slaves to sin, who do not have peace and who do not know where they will be going when they die. Someone needs to share with them the Good

News. The world needs a whole lot more pastors, prophets, apostles, evangelists and teachers, to share the Word of God.

As believers we should financially support those who serve in teaching the word of God and ministering to us in spiritual matters. There are many ministers who serve God but who are unable to support their own families. There are also many believers who did not answer the call to serve as full time ministers because they were afraid they would not have enough money to support themselves and would need to rely on the church for support. There are many who are anointed but not able to fully utilize their gift because of financial constraints. Therefore it is crucial that those who are not full time ministers succeed in life so they can help financially support those in ministry. When a youth succeeds, his family prospers and the church's influence expands.

Ministers need to empower their congregation by explaining the word of God in relevant way so that youth are able to apply biblical wisdom in their school, work or business lives. One of the challenges the youth face today is they are not able to apply what they learned on Sunday to school on Monday. The youth need practical, strong, relevant messages that do not water down the gospel of Jesus Christ. Unfortunately many youth abandon their faith when they get to college because they did not have a strong foundation of faith to begin with, so they are not able to defend it when confronted by questions that are raised by atheist professors or unbelievers. The church needs to be a preparing and a refueling ground for the next genera-tion so they can go out and change the world. The church will need to raise Christ like Christians who will solve problems, influence the world and who are a light in the darkness.

Salvation prayer

If you have never made a decision to accept Christ as your Savior, please consider praying the prayer after the table.

When you make this very important decision, the table below shows you some of the change that will transpire in your life:

Verse	Before Accepting Christ	After Accepting Christ
John 1:12	Not a child of God	Child of God
John 3:16	Eternal Death	For God so loved the world that He gave His only begotten Son, that whoever believes in Him should not perish but have everlasting life.
Ephesians 5:8	You were once darkness	You are light in the Lord
Romans 6:17-18	Slave to sin	Slave to righteousness
Colossians 1: 21-22	Once were alienated and enemies in your mind by wicked works	He has reconciled in the body of His flesh through death, to present you holy, and blameless, and above reproach in His sight
Galatians 3:29	No inheritance	Abraham's seed, and heirs according to the promise
2 Corinthians 5:17	Fallen creature	Therefore if any man be in Christ, he is a new creature: old things are passed away; behold, all things are become new.

1 Corinthians 3:16	Holy Spirit is not within you	Do you not know that you are the temple of God and that the Spirit of God dwells in you?
1 Peter 2:24	No covenant for healing	Who Himself bore our sins in His own body on the tree, that we, having died to sins, might live for righteousness—by whose stripes you were healed.
Ephesians 2:1	Dead in trespasses and sins	Made alive
Ephesians 2:2-10	You once walked according to the course of this world, according to the prince of the power of the air, the spirit who now works in the sons of disobedience, among whom also we all once conducted ourselves in the lusts of our flesh, fulfilling the desires of the flesh and of the mind, and were by nature children of wrath, just as the others.	Alive together with Christ (by grace you have been saved), and raised us up together, and made us sit together in the heavenly places in Christ Jesus, that in the ages to come He might show the exceeding riches of His grace in His kindness toward us in Christ Jesus. For we are His workmanship, created in Christ Jesus for good works, which God prepared beforehand that we should walk in them.
Ephesians 2: 12-13	Strangers from the covenants of promise, having no hope and without God in the world	But now in Christ Jesus you who once were far off have been brought near by the blood of Christ.

Salvation Prayer

God your word says in Romans 10: 9-10 (NKJV)

"that if you confess with your mouth the Lord Jesus and believe in your heart that God has raised Him from the dead, you will be saved. For with the heart one believes unto righteousness, and with the mouth confession is made unto salvation."

And according to your word I confess with my mouth

Jesus is Lord and I believe in my heart that God has raised Him from the dead.

God forgive all my sins.

I thank you because of this confession that I am saved and I have become your child.

I receive everything Jesus Christ has accomplished on the cross.

I receive the eternal life, righteousness, healing, peace, prosperity,

and the authority I have as your child.

I also receive the Holy Spirit you have sent to guide and comfort us.

I pray this in Jesus Name.

Date:_____

CREATION IS WAITING FOR YOU!

CREATION IS WAITING FOR YOU!

References

[1] Atta-Asamoah, Andrews & Severino, Jean-Michelle. BBC. 2014. "Head-to-head: Is Africa's young population a risk or an asset?" http://www.bbc.com/news/world-africa-25869838 (Accessed 2015-11-1).

[2] The Guardian. 2014. Global youth heatmap. http://www.theguardian.com/world/graphic/2014/mar/19/world-map-of-youth-youth-bulge?CMP=twt_gu (Accessed 2015-11-1).

[3] Central Intelligence Agency. The World Fact Book. https://www.cia.gov/library/publications/the-world-factbook/geos/et.html. (Accessed 2015-11-1).

[4] (MENTOR, 2009; Cavell, DuBois, Karcher, Keller, & Rhodes, 2009). http://youth.gov/youth-topics/mentoring/benefits-mentoring-young-people#sthash.Nk141BSX.dpuf (Accessed 2015-11-1).

[5] Watt, Louise. China to end decades –old 1-child policy, allow 2 children. Yahoo. 10-29-2015. http://news.yahoo.com/china-decides-abolish-1-child-policy-allow-2-110127816.html (Accessed 2015-11-1).